Activities to Promote
Critical Thinking

Activities to Promote Critical Thinking

Classroom Practices in Teaching English, 1986

Jeff Golub, Chair,
and the Committee on Classroom Practices

National Council of Teachers of English
1111 Kenyon Road, Urbana, Illinois 61801

Grateful acknowledgment is made for permission to reprint the following material: Duck-rabbit illustration from *Philosophical Investigations*, 3d ed., by Ludwig Wittgenstein, Macmillan, 1970. Reproduced with permission of Basil Blackwell Limited, Oxford. Hidden word puzzle from *Fun and Tricks for Young Scientists* by George Barr, McGraw-Hill, 1968. Reproduced with permission of author. Excerpt from "The Gift of Life" by Phillip Doughtie from *Understanding Human Communication* by Ronald B. Adler and George R. Rodman, Holt, Rinehart and Winston, 1985. Reprinted with permission. Excerpt from "The Caffein Concern" by Christine Murphy from *The Art of Public Speaking*, edited by Stephen E. Lucas, Random House, 1983. Reprinted with permission. Excerpt from "I Have a Dream" by Martin Luther King, Jr. Copyright © 1963 by Martin Luther King, Jr. Reprinted wtih permission of Joan Daves. Jigsaw puzzles from *Fun with Puzzles* by Joseph Leeming, J. B. Lippincott, 1946. Reproduced with permission.

Staff Editor: Jane M. Curran

Book Design: Tom Kovacs for TGK Design

NCTE Stock Number 00457

Library of Congress Cataloging in Publication Data

Activities to promote critical thinking.

    Includes bibliographies.
    1. English philology—Study and teaching.   2. English
language—Composition and exercises—Study and teaching.
3. English language—Rhetoric—Study and teaching.
4. Thought and thinking—Study and teaching.   5. Creative
thinking (Education). 6. Language arts. I. Golub, Jeff.
II. National Council of Teachers of English. Committee
on Classroom Practices.
PE66.A33   1986   428'.007'1   86-21741
ISBN 0-8141-0045-7

Contents

Introduction

Each November the members of the Committee on Classroom Practices in Teaching English meet at the NCTE Annual Convention to select a topic for the next issue of the yearly publication. We listen to those teachers in attendance at our session; we try to gauge the kinds of topics receiving the most treatment and emphasis in recent journals; we imagine what new developments and changes are likely to occur next year.

Finally, we pick a pertinent topic that we think teachers might want to know more about; we issue a call for manuscripts on this topic that suggest practical, immediately usable classroom strategies; and then we send the submitted papers to each of the six Classroom Practices Committee members for review and evaluation. This year, ninety contributions were submitted, and the Classroom Practices Committee selected thirty. These thirty were submitted to the five-member NCTE Editorial Board, which has the final approval for publication, as it does for every NCTE publication.

Some years it is difficult to decide what instructional or professional issue is currently of most concern to teachers. But 1984 was different: the topic we wanted was readily apparent. We could see it in the journals that devoted increasingly more space to articles dealing with the development of students' creative and critical thinking skills; we saw it in the decision at NCTE Headquarters to publish student texts entitled *Thinking through Language;* and we were reminded of the NCTE document titled "Essentials of English," especially the section on Thinking Skills:

> Because thinking and language are closely linked, teachers of English have always held that one of their main duties is to teach students *how* to think. Thinking skills, involved in the study of all disciplines, are inherent in the reading, writing, speaking, listening and observing involved in the study of English. The ability to analyze, classify, compare, formulate hypotheses, make inferences, and draw conclusions is essential to the reasoning processes of all adults. The capacity to solve problems, both rationally and intuitively, is a way to help students cope successfully with the experience of learning within the school setting and outside.

Echoing this priority were the comments of teachers at the 1984 NCTE Convention. They were well aware of the trend toward an emphasis on students' thinking skills, but they were concerned about *how* to implement such an instructional approach.

If it is true that "Good teaching is knowing the available options," then this present volume might be of some help to those teachers who want to find additional ways to involve their students in projects that encourage (or even require) creative and critical thinking. Do not be misled by the title of this book, however. We are not dealing with instructional approaches that put aside the usual focus on reading and writing and speaking and listening skills so that one can concentrate instead on *thinking*. Rather, we present here articles describing methods that involve students in language and communication study in such a way that *significant thinking occurs*. The authors in this publication have not moved away from the study of literature or the improvement of students' writing skills; instead, they outline ways to teach literature and composition that engage the students in such thinking processes as these: inferring, sequencing, relating, classifying, organizing, predicting, confirming, questioning, analyzing, synthesizing, imagining, problem solving, and evaluating.

One more indication of the strength of this trend toward an emphasis on students' thinking skills is the large number of manuscripts submitted in response to our call. Ninety papers were received from educators at all levels of instruction, all of which were read by each of the committee members: Patricia Phelan, Carlota Cárdenas de Dwyer, Beverly Busching, Joe Milner, Jane Hornburger, and Jay Lalley. We tried to select the most insightful, innovative, and articulate presentations of practical classroom strategies designed to develop students' creative, logical, and critical thinking skills.

The committee members and I sincerely hope that you will find the ideas presented here to be of real value to you in your teaching.

Jeff Golub
Shorecrest High School
Seattle, Washington

1 Composition Activities

Using the Poetic Voice to Teach Story Forms and Writing in the Elementary Grades

Raymond Bailey
North Evanston Elementary School, Evanston, Wyoming

A major difficulty which most teachers encounter is getting young children to write or to tell a story. "What shall I write about?" is often the response; sadly and more often, "I don't know any" ends the child's attempt. We blame the failure on children's lack of creativity or interest and despair of their ever resolving the problem of writer's block. But the problem, I have discovered, comes largely from our own use of language. Without the appropriate language to introduce the proper mood, who does not blanch at the prospect of having to produce something creative at a moment's notice?

Picture Narration

In working with children of varying age and ability, I have found that my own choice of language largely determines the responses I get, especially from young children. For example, I approached six-year-old Dara, who was carefully drawing an elaborate picture.

"Tell me about your picture," I asked.

"Well, there's a castle, and a princess," she replied. "And there's a guard and some birds flying. That's all."

In truth she had done as I had asked. The result was curiously like the unfocused chain which characterizes children's primitive narratives (Applebee 1978). In these, children will usually provide a random string or list of information in response to a request.

"Fine," I said. "Now let me tell you a story about that picture." I then made up a story with characters, action, and dialogue that might fit within the scheme of what I saw in the picture and what Dara had described.

3

Dara was delighted. When I asked if she could tell me a story about the picture, she produced the following, which I transcribed as she spoke:

> There was a princess who lived in a castle and there was a guard who loved her. And he would fight every day against the prince. The prince just wants to get rid of the knight so he can get the princess to be his wife. And the prince was always after the eagles that the princess liked to watch. The end.

How very different this response is to the initial comments produced when I merely asked Dara to tell me about her picture! By providing a story about *her* picture, which was something she knew about and produced, I was able to inspire her to become more open with me and to contribute her own imaginative version of what she had drawn. The pleasure she derived from being a spectator to a story, the setting of which she had provided, allowed her to relax and enjoy another's efforts; then she was sufficiently motivated to produce her own version.

Moving from the Expressive Voice to the Poetic Voice

James Britton (1970) defines two aspects of language use: first, the expressive voice, which we use spontaneously with our families and friends and which encompasses aspects of thought, emotions, and everyday events; and second, the poetic voice, which is more highly structured and akin to narrative. One readily recognizes certain conventions such as "Once upon a time," "lived happily ever after," and "The end" in these narratives and, in addition, a more heightened use of expression in terms of simile and metaphor, as well as setting, character, dialogue, and action.

Dara's second version is an example of her moving from the expressive voice to the poetic voice, in which she manages to include some of the more obvious conventions of story form. Remarkably, she transforms mere birds to "eagles that the princess liked to watch" and includes them in the action of the story. However, this change from the expressive to the poetic voice was largely instigated by the creation of an appropriate mood through my own use of that voice. Another factor was Dara's knowledge of story form, which she had learned both at home and in school.

Enhancing the Meaning of a Story

Telling stories in the poetic voice is difficult because of the formal structure that is demanded. Britton (1970) points out the importance of the spectator role in reaching an understanding of the poetic mode and suggests that it is *assimilative*. Assimilation is, essentially, the means through which new experience is given meaning. As each experience is encountered, it is incorporated within a framework that provides the meaning and thus broadens our understanding of events with each new experience.

All experience is construed by individuals on a personal level. This is true whether the event is experienced in the real world or from the spectator role. It is, therefore, all the more important for teachers not only to tell stories but also to include within them aspects of the children's daily lives. The immediacy of using children's names and incorporating everyday events, such as birthdays or holidays, undoubtedly increases the effectiveness of the story. When personal interest is involved, all teaching becomes more effective. This becomes even more important when we expect higher-level thinking skills to be applied either in reaction to stories or in the elicitation of other stories.

The effectiveness of the stories is also enhanced by the inclusion of a dramatic interpretation in which the teacher or storyteller uses changes in accent and voice pitch to delineate different characters and their qualities. There is no doubt that such a dramatic rendition, complete with appropriate prosodic attributes (pauses, intonation, rhythm, and inflections), contributes not only to the enjoyment of the tale, but also to the overall comprehension of its intent (Bailey 1983).

Group Story Writing

Once children have mastered the conventions of stories, I encourage them to participate in the story-making process with me. I ask third, fourth, and fifth graders to contribute their ideas and reactions as well as their feelings and judgments about a story I make up. For example, I might tell them that it has been a long time since I was a child and that I no longer remember clearly my reactions to specific encounters. Then I seek their help in making the story more real. Using an overhead projector, I write part of a story, introducing the characters and the setting and initiating the action. We discuss these elements and the initial action. I make changes as I incorporate some of their ideas into the story.

The purpose of this group story writing is to broaden children's understanding of stories and to teach them that writing is a process which can undergo many changes until it sounds consistent and real. This activity also helps children organize information and ideas, analyze characters and their actions, maintain linear thought, and make judgments concerning the whole. Inevitably, it also enhances their comprehension of the stories they read.

Once I get to a critical point in the story, I look for suggestions as to what could or will happen next. At this time I distribute copies of the partial story, and we all write an ending to the story. If the story is good and has excited the class, I will eventually get a page or several pages from children who hitherto would produce only an isolated fragment or two. When the completed versions are collected, the class discusses each ending and incorporates aspects of the narratives into a final version. I take care to ensure that each child makes a contribution to the class story so that every child will recognize his or her contribution when I hand out copies of the final version.

Improving Self-Esteem

These activities are not bound by any curricular spectrum; they provide lessons in storytelling, reading, comprehension, spelling, punctuation, writing, and critical and comparative thinking. In addition, there is the immeasurable confidence and self-esteem that each child gains in contributing to a process which he or she can see grow and take shape. This understanding leads, in turn, to a positive self-concept and improved performance in other areas of classroom learning; it may inspire students to compete in school and independent writing projects sponsored by local and state parent-teacher groups and by reading councils of the International Reading Association.

Most children who fall behind in reading and writing do so not because of a lack of intelligence, but through a lack of experience with story forms and with language interaction and through the failure to achieve initial success. Traditional workbook exercises will never compensate for this. Active modeling by the teacher and similar productions by the children in a positive partnership can give students that initial success and can help them realize that writing is neither hard nor futile but is, rather, a rewarding and exciting experience.

References

Applebee, Arthur N. *The Child's Concept of Story: Ages Two to Seventeen*. Chicago: University of Chicago Press, 1978.

Bailey, Raymond. "Speech Prosody as a Teaching Device: Does Reading Fluency Improve?" Ph.D. diss., University of Virginia, 1983.

Britton, James N. *Language and Learning*. London: Allen Lane, 1970.

The Metaphor as a Metaphor for English Class

Carole B. Bencich
Brevard County Schools, Rockledge, Florida

The metaphor, a source of vitality in both literature and common speech, is also a product of analogous thinking, and should be taught as such. Activities which reinforce metaphorical thought will encourage students to associate familiar objects, places, people, or concepts with new ideas. Practice in metaphor making puts students in contact with their own thinking habits and unites their powers of imagination and analysis. It gives young people a new way of interpreting their environment and their experiences. It helps them recognize the role of metaphors in literature; and, finally, it leads to improvement in writing style.

Metaphor making fulfills many useful functions in the classroom. It provides a way of synthesizing the abstract concepts of literary study. It activates students' memory by involving them with content, and it taps the creative potential of the right brain. Used on a regular basis by teacher and students alike, the metaphor can become a *leitmotiv* for English class.

Introducing Metaphors

Adolescent slang abounds in metaphorical thought, a fact which makes the concept easy to introduce in class. From the irreverence of nicknames like "Moose" and "Freckles" to the casual phrases "It's a breeze" or "He burned me," students delight in their own inventive expressions. Since spoken language also includes many stale comparisons, the teacher might begin by identifying these expressions and refurbishing them for effective use. Discuss the meanings and possible origins of such terms as "mad as a wet hen," "cute as a button," or "go the distance," and ask students to write new versions which express the same idea. For a research project, or ongoing classroom enrichment, consult Stuart B. Flexner's *Listening to America: An Illustrated History of*

Words and Phrases from Our Lively and Splendid Past (Simon and Schuster, 1982) or other dictionaries of slang.

Students enjoy making a game of inventing metaphors. With the teacher establishing a category, like *cars* or *musical instruments* or *vegetables*, young people will readily identify a character in a novel as "a Buick," "a French horn," or "a squash." They will just as readily apply metaphors to objects, ideas, literary periods, novels, or even each other's compositions. After all, "Your paper reminded me of a waltz" gives a writer a meaningful overall perception of tone or style. This game also teaches students how to extend a metaphor. After deciding "He is a machine," for instance, a writer could extend that comparison into "He is a robot, programmed to perform the same functions over and over again, with no thought or sensitivity to the people around him." Beginning in simplistic play, this activity develops comparative thinking skills, provides synthesis of abstract concepts, and integrates language and personal experience.

Active discussion remains one of the best ways to share different thinking processes and thus broaden students' repertoire of strategies. When students generate a metaphor, they should describe what unfamiliar or fresh insight they are contributing to a familiar subject. What emotional or imaginative qualities are being ascribed? What is the contrast between the idea expressed and the image by which it is expressed? Is it an obvious connection, a subtle thought link, or an artificial device? Does the metaphor add significance to the idea, or is it mere "decoration"? When students share the thinking behind their metaphors, they discover a wide range of associations and responses among their peers.

At this early stage of awareness about metaphors, students are able to apply the concept to themselves in a visual way. Ask them to make a poster of original artwork or a collage of pictures from magazines to represent visually a brief metaphor about themselves. Give them plenty of examples, such as the following eighth-grade products:

> I am undiscovered gold, lying in the hills.
> Just wait until the world discovers me!
>
> I am a grape, just one of the bunch,
> but with my own juicy goodness.
>
> I am a pawn, moved around by others,
> but without me the game wouldn't work.

The visual and expressive elements of this project make it highly motivational, and it is also appropriate for students of all ability levels. The finished products make an impressive classroom display.

To focus attention on comparative thought, present a "metaphor for the day." Read aloud, or post on the bulletin board, a successful metaphor gleaned from your own reading or, better, from students' papers. Have students scout for metaphors in outside reading and bring them to class. Comic strips and newspaper sports stories offer many examples. Establish criteria for an effective metaphor (striking, appropriate, etc.) and ask individuals to rank the daily metaphor on a scale of 1 to 10, with explanation.

Further Activities with Metaphors

Increased awareness of metaphoric thought will help students when they encounter figurative language in literature. When Stephen Crane compares the "small procession of wounded men" to "a flow of blood from the torn body of the brigade," stop and examine *how* that metaphor works (as opposed to what it means). Let students name all the ways a group of men can be like a flow of blood. Ask them to visualize the procession, perhaps setting the scene for a movie camera shot. Consider other ways in which Crane might have expressed a similar image or concept. With sufficient practice in "easy" contexts, more subtle metaphors, like "the road not taken," become keys rather than obstacles to understanding.

Using metaphors as thought links can help young writers focus their thinking into a composition topic. High school students, still needing to write in the expressive mode but required to write transactional papers for various assignments, can use metaphoric thinking to get started. Show them how to force association between the familiar and unfamiliar by asking students to make a list of five subjects with which they are familiar (for example, *surfing, rock music, pizza, cars,* and *video games*). Then give them a list of five broad "English" subjects such as *Emerson, freedom, poetry, the epic hero,* and *conflict.* Students then must link each of their five personal subjects with one of the broader subjects and write a topic sentence which logically connects the two. The teacher should demonstrate several examples on the chalkboard first. For instance, *surfing* might be combined with *freedom* in "Surfers understand the fullest meaning of the word *freedom.*" Although *rock music* and *epic hero* might be integrated in an interesting sentence, *poetry* and *video games* might prove impossible. Working through such a list orally with students will produce varied results. The topic sentences resulting from such practice should seldom be developed into a composition. However, this activity will teach a young writer to channel an expressive voice into the requirements of the academic assignment.

Gabriele Rico's technique of clustering will also foster metaphor-making ability. Give students a word or a concept and ask them to cluster metaphors for three or four minutes. For instance, *Mark Twain* might produce the following cluster:

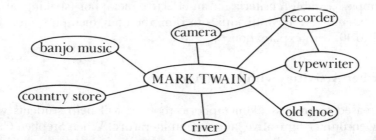

In all cases, students should be asked to explain how the metaphor works. For example, "Mark Twain is like banjo music because he's folksy, easy to listen to, and improvises as he tells a story." No one answer is ever the "right" metaphor, but students benefit from hearing the different ways of thinking represented by varying metaphors. The object is to extend thinking, to expand the power of language beyond its denotative limits.

Metaphors will also help students prepare persuasive arguments. Political rhetoric is rich in metaphoric comparisons, some of which are overused to the point of satire (e.g., *cancer, poison, team*). Students need to learn how to use this reasoning in their own arguments. They need to learn how to choose appropriate and effective metaphors, and how to extend images without mixing impressions.

By beginning with vivid examples of metaphors in literature and speech and by capitalizing on students' pleasure in making metaphors which add dimension to an ordinary subject, the teacher is reinforcing students' ability to think by analogy. Ultimately, this ability will aid students in interpreting new material, as well as in expressing their own ideas. Adoption of the metaphor as a metaphor for English class will communicate the need for imaginative links between the familiar and the unfamiliar. It will require the active participation of comparative thought and the shared insights of multiple interpretations.

Writing a Thesis Statement: A Right-Brain Activity

Carolyn Boiarsky
Illinois State University, Normal

One of the major reasons many students have so much difficulty writing a thesis sentence is that it involves the synthesizing of information, a skill which few of them have mastered and a skill for which they have had little training. It is a skill which requires an inductive leap from a vast amount of information to a single, overall concept. This thinking process is the second highest level of cognitive learning on Bloom's taxonomic scale and is identified as the province of the right brain by Ronald Rubenzer, the founder of Thinking Dynamics in Greensboro, North Carolina. How can we teachers foster the development of this important skill?

During the past three years I have been helping students at Illinois Central College (a two-year community college) and at Georgia Institute of Technology and nuclear engineers in high-tech industries learn to synthesize information into a single, coherent concept which serves as a thesis statement. The following curriculum provides a sequence of lessons which leads students through the steps required to synthesize information and arrive at a thesis sentence. While the lessons have been developed for students at the college level, they are applicable to all levels and can be adapted to classes at the upper elementary, middle, and secondary levels.

The lessons are divided into two phases. During Phase I the class works as a group to write a thesis statement for a single assignment. During Phase II the students work individually on an assignment. Both assignments are centered around advertising techniques and can be tied into a unit on advertising.

Phase I

The class is given the following assignment:

> You are an executive with a large company. The contract with the A.B.C. Advertising Agency is coming up for renewal. Your com-

11

pany has decided not to renew the contract and is in the process of looking for a new agency to represent it. Your company has narrowed the search to two agencies. An ad by one of these agencies is attached to this assignment. Mr. Osgood, your boss and company vice president, has asked you to analyze this ad and to write him a memo explaining how the agency uses various techniques to advertise the product. He will use your analysis to determine if the agency can develop an effective ad for your company.

Any magazine ad can be used. I often use cigarette or car ads, or computer ads for my engineering students.

In order for the students to formulate a thesis statement for the memo which they are to write, they will need to perform the following six steps.

1. Identify Purpose and Audience

Because a thesis statement needs to relate to the purpose and audience of a piece of discourse, students need to determine these two aspects. For this particular assignment the students usually conclude the following:

> *Purpose:* to determine whether the advertising agency uses effective techniques.
>
> *Audience:* Mr. Osgood, our boss and company vice president.

2. Gather Information

Students are urged to gather as much information as they can about the ad, without worrying about whether it is relevant or meaningful. This step and the following four steps are conducted in the form of brainstorming sessions, with students calling out ideas and the teacher recording their responses on the chalkboard in abbreviated fashion. For example, when my students analyzed an ad for MCI, the long-distance telephone service, they listed much of the following information:

> a single picture
>
> a lot of copy
>
> the name of the company is in large letters
>
> a box lets you send for more information
>
> a picture of a man holding his fingers in his ears

a long headline

information about customers using the company

a picture of a man looking upset

the name of a competitor in the headline

a play on words in the headline

information about the cost

the cost is cheaper than the competition

information about the WATS line

information about billing

information about savings for businesses

a picture of a businessman

the word *business* in the headline

a play on words in the copy

3. Find Relationships among the Pieces of Information

Students are asked to look at their descriptive list to see which pieces of information are related to each other. In the example of the MCI ad, there are several pieces of information which relate to the use of a picture; others relate to the competitor; still others to businesses. Some pieces of information, like the box for requesting further information, don't seem to be related to anything else; others, like information about the cost of the service, may fit into two or more groups of information. As students call out the relationships, I usually mark them with different symbols. For example, I may give one category an asterisk, another a check, and a third an *x*. When the students finish, the list usually looks like this:

*   a single picture
/   a lot of copy
    the name of the company in large letters
    a box lets you send for more information
*   a picture of a man holding his fingers in his ears
/   a long headline
o   information about customers using the company
*   a picture of a man looking upset
/# the name of a competitor in the headline
√/ a play on words in the headline

o   information about the cost

#o   the cost is cheaper than the competition

o   information about the WATS line

o   information about billing

xo   information about savings for businesses

*x   a picture of a businessman

/x   the word *business* in the headline

√/   a play on words in the copy

4. Categorize the Relationships

At this point I recopy the list, putting the related items together. Students then should determine an identifying name for each of the categories of information. I usually place the name they select at the side of each category, so the listing looks like this:

a single picture
a picture of a man holding his ears   ⎤
a picture of a man looking upset   ⎬ Photography
a picture of a businessman   ⎦

a lot of copy
a long headline
the name of a competitor in the headline   ⎤
a play on words in the headline   ⎬ Copy
the word *business* in the headline
a play on words in the copy   ⎦

information about customers using the company ⎤
information about the cost
information about the WATS line   ⎬ General
information about billing   information
information about savings for businesses   ⎦

the name of a competitor in the headline   ⎤
the cost is cheaper than the competition   ⎬ Competition

a play on words in the headline   ⎤
a play on words in the copy   ⎬ Wordplay

information about savings for businesses

a picture of a businessman   ⎤ — Business

the word *business* in the headline   ⎦

5. Write an Assertion for Each Category

An assertion is a sentence that establishes a relationship among pieces of information (Van Nostrand et al. 1982). Determining these assertions forces students to verbalize a complete thought about each category. Students suggested the following assertions for the six categories:

Photography: A large photograph pictures a businessman holding his ears in pain.

Copy: The copy for the headline and the rest of the page attracts the reader's attention.

General information: The copy tells a lot of information about MCI.

The competition: The ad compares AT&T with MCI.

Wordplay: The agency plays with words to catch the reader's attention.

Business: The ad focuses on the businessman's needs.

I usually record these assertions on the board under each category. Often students suggest several assertions for each category, which I record if they state a relationship concerning the information in each of the categories. Only after all of the assertions are recorded do we attempt to narrow the list down to a single statement for each category. This may mean eliminating all but one of the assertions, or it may mean combining two or more into a single new statement.

6. Determine an Organizing Idea

The Organizing Idea (O.I.) is an assertion which unifies the other assertions (Van Nostrand et al. 1982). It is the central idea around which all other assertions are related. Students look at the various assertions for each of the categories and then derive an O.I., a single assertion which will be broad enough to incorporate all the assertions.

Often students will suggest several possible O.I.'s. As with the assertions, all O.I.'s should be recorded. Then have students go back and refine the list to a single O.I. Often they will decide to combine ideas from several suggested O.I.'s to create a new O.I.

Students in one class, after numerous revisions, derived the following O.I.: "The advertising agency effectively conveys the message that MCI offers better services to businesses than AT&T does."

Once students have determined an O.I., they can work together to draft the introductory paragraph of the paper. The O.I. will serve as the thesis statement. It does not have to be the first sentence, though it often is. Here are two different paragraphs which use the same O.I.

1. The advertising agency is effectively conveying to the audience that MCI offers better services to businesses than AT&T does. The agency achieves this by using striking photography, a catchy headline, and information-packed copy.

2. The man is obviously a businessman and he is holding his ears in pain. According to the headline, it's because he has "heard enough." Of AT&T that is. The ad agency has effectively conveyed to the reader that MCI offers better services to businesses than AT&T.

Phase II

At this point students are ready to write on their own. The second assignment is related to the first and allows students to build on what they have already done. I give them the following directions.

> Now that you have analyzed an ad by one of the advertising agencies which your company is considering, your boss, Mr. Osgood, would like you to look at an ad which the other advertising agency wrote. Mr. Osgood has asked you to analyze this ad and then to determine which ad you feel is better. He has asked you to write him a memo which recommends one of the advertising agencies over the other, based on the techniques used in the ads.

This time students receive an ad for a similar product or service offered by a different company. If I start with an ad for MCI, I next give students an ad for AT&T.

Students follow the six steps in Phase I to analyze the second ad. They usually have little difficulty arriving at a thesis statement or Organizing Idea which indicates a preference for one agency over the other. A sample student O.I. would read: "The MCI ad is superior since it is more informative, gives a more complete sales pitch, and is more impressive visually than the AT&T ad."

To encourage students to follow all six steps in the analysis, I have them complete the worksheet shown in Figure 1. I also have students use the self-evaluation form shown in Figure 2 to analyze the first drafts of their memos to Mr. Osgood. The form helps them spot where revisions are needed.

Phase II Worksheet

Purpose: What do I hope to accomplish?

Audience: Who is my reader? What does the reader need to know? What do I know about the reader?

Information: Jot down data about your subject.

Relationships: Look for links between your information fragments.

Categories: Name each of the groups of relationships.

Assertions: Write a complete sentence for each category.

Organizing Idea: Write an assertion which is broad enough to cover all of your other assertions.

Figure 1. Sample worksheet for Phase II assignment.

Evaluation Sheet

Rate your performance in each area by circling *Yes* or *No*, or the appropriate number from 1 (poor or inadequate) to 5 (excellent).

1. Do I have an O.I. (and only one) per paragraph? — Yes   No

2. Is the O.I. the most comprehensive assertion? — Yes   No

3. Is the O.I. clearly and explicitly stated? — 1 2 3 4 5

4. Do all the other assertions support or clarify the O.I. (no redundant or irrelevant information included)? — 1 2 3 4 5

5. Is there enough supporting detail to convince my reader to accept my O.I. and for my reader to understand (no relevant detail omitted)? — 1 2 3 4 5

6. Do all my sentences flow smoothly into each other? — 1 2 3 4 5

7. Is my language appropriate? — 1 2 3 4 5

Figure 2. Sample self-evaluation form for Phase II assignment.

Expanding the Assignment

Once students have completed the two phases in the advertising unit, they are ready to apply the techniques to an entirely new topic. They might be asked to analyze a character in a book they are reading or to prepare a brief research paper on a current topic, such as legislation requiring the use of seat belts. As students apply the six steps for synthesizing information to other assignments, their papers become more organized and coherent. By combining this right-brain activity with the left-brain activities in which they are often drilled, students can learn to write effective papers with viable thesis statements.

Reference

Van Nostrand, A. D., C. H. Knoblauch, and Joan Pettigrew. *The Process of Writing: Discovery and Control.* 2d ed. Boston: Houghton Mifflin, 1982.

Justice Is a Nike T-Shirt: Using Synectics in the ESL Writing Class

Nancy Pfingstag
University of North Carolina at Charlotte

The need to teach cognitive skills in the writing class has been well documented. As Taylor (1981), Flower and Hayes (1981), and Zamel (1984) have argued, writing is a thinking skill, a process of discovering and exploring meaning. The prewriting activity described here is a procedure which teaches students one way to think about extended definitions of abstract concepts in order to formulate, clarify, organize, and communicate their ideas in written form. This activity is termed *synectic* because the student compares an abstract to a concrete object which is chosen at random. The metaphor that is generated and developed is a product of the student's imagination and creativity.

Synectic metaphors are most successful in advanced ESL writing classes because of the level of English required to handle abstractions. The following description is based on five fifty-minute classes.

Day 1

The activity begins by having students brainstorm to identify as many abstract terms as possible. Because students often have initial difficulty generating terms, I start a working list by writing words such as *honesty* and *bravery* on the chalkboard. I explain briefly that an abstract term is something that cannot be perceived by the senses or captured in a container (like oxygen).

The students and I then each select one of the terms to be used as the subject of an extended definition essay. In one class, I selected *justice;* Daniel, a young man from the People's Republic of China, chose *pride*. After the terms have been chosen and entered into our journals, we set the journals aside temporarily.

Day 2

I bring to class a grab bag containing a collection of objects put together
haphazardly. I purposely try not to choose objects for their special
qualities, as even the most mundane object, if studied closely, can be
fascinating and worthy of serious attention. Currently, my grab bag
contains such things as a man's tie, a stapler, a mushroom-shaped
candle, and a coupon offering a front-end wheel alignment for $16.67.
The students and I each reach into the bag and pull out the first object
we touch—no fishing around is allowed. The object I pulled from the
bag was a Nike-brand T-shirt; Daniel grabbed a 3M-brand tape
dispenser.

We next inspect our objects carefully, noting the different parts and
their purposes. At this stage, I begin modeling each step of the
prewriting activity for the students as we work along together. By
listening to me think aloud and following my different drafts, the class
can observe and practice the strategies for generating ideas, sorting out
thoughts, and organizing information that I have chosen to
demonstrate.

As I examined the Nike T-shirt aloud, I decided that it had five
major parts: *front, back, sleeves, seams,* and *label.* I listed these across the
chalkboard, leaving ample "thinking" space below each part. I then
focused on each part separately. As I described what I observed and
as I determined a purpose for each quality, I wrote my thoughts on the
chalkboard in the appropriate columns, as shown in Table 1. I noticed
that the front of the shirt was made of soft, stretchy material which
made it comfortable to wear. The bright red Nike symbol, a bold
checklike stroke connoting the speed and accuracy of the Greek victory
goddess Nike, undoubtedly made a statement about the values and
beliefs of the wearer of the shirt. I found that the back of the shirt was
plain and could not be distinguished from the back of any other white
T-shirt. The sleeves were short, allowing freedom of movement, and
hemmed, which gave the shirt a neat appearance. The seams were
double-stitched inside the shirt to keep the pieces from coming apart.
The double-stitching probably made the consumer feel confident that
the shirt was worth the price. The label, I discovered, offered an
abundance of information. Sewn securely into the shirt for safekeeping,
it gave instructions on the care of the T-shirt and important data on
the size of the shirt and its fiber content.

When all of this information was on the chalkboard, the students
and I discussed the qualities of the shirt that I had identified. I
explained that when I had difficulty determining the purpose of a

Table 1

Nike T-Shirt

Front	Label
Material is soft, stretchy	Sewn into the neck seam
feels comfortable	easily found
adjusts to the body	stays attached to shirt
Material is white	Gives size of shirt
attractive color	information about fit
sets off Nike symbol	general size (large) and
implies purity, cleanliness	specific size (42/44)
goes with all colors	Gives washing instructions
Red Nike symbol	allows person to give proper
connotes speed, victory,	care to shirt
freedom	informs as to what is
makes a statement about	harmful (do not bleach)
wearer's values and beliefs	Gives fiber content
calls attention to wearer	100% cotton
	shirt will "breathe"

Back	Sleeves	Seams
No design or pattern	Sleeves are short	Sewn inside the shirt
makes no statement	allows for freedom of movement	creates a neat appearance
cannot be distinguished from any other T-shirt back	keeps wearer cool	keeps seams from being obvious
very practical	Sleeves are hemmed	Double-stitched
	creates a neat appearance	keeps pieces from coming apart
	keeps threads from raveling	gives confidence to consumer

particular quality, I had to rely on my assumptions. For example, I did not know if double-stitching made other consumers feel confident, but since it made me feel that way, I assumed other consumers were also concerned about stitching quality.

Day 3

The students inspect their individual objects, determining the parts and purposes. In their journals, they form a grid similar to the one I placed on the chalkboard the previous day. As they study and examine, I move around the classroom in order to answer questions or to prompt a student who is having difficulty looking at the object from a different perspective.

As shown in Table 2, Daniel divided his 3M tape dispenser into four parts: *dispenser, roll of tape, disk in the center of the tape,* and *cutting edge.* He noticed that the dispenser was made of inexpensive plastic, a modern material which probably saved the 3M Company money. The roll of tape had an undetermined amount of tape on it since part of the roll had been used. He found this irritating because he would be unable to estimate whether he had sufficient tape to complete a project. The disk, Daniel found, allowed the tape to pull smoothly and kept the user from becoming frustrated. The cutting edge was made of metal, for strength.

After the students have completed their grids, they return the objects to the grab bag, retaining only their written thoughts about the objects.

Day 4

The students are asked to turn back in their journals to the abstract term they chose on Day 1. I then write the incomplete sentence "[abstract term] is a [object]" on the chalkboard. The students write the statement in their journals, filling in the appropriate information. For example, my statement read, "Justice is a Nike T-shirt." Daniel's was "Pride is a 3M tape dispenser." Other statements in the class were "Love is a Christmas ornament," "Beauty is a bottle of Bufferin," and "Peace is a two-in-one can opener."

Once again, I draw a grid on the chalkboard and write down the different parts of my grab-bag object. In the example of the Nike T-shirt and justice, I wrote on the board the following categories: *front, back, sleeves, seams, label.* As I concentrated on each part of the shirt, I referred back to my notes from Day 2 and asked myself how an aspect

Table 2

3M Tape Dispenser

Dispenser	Roll of Tape

Color is clear
   you can see the tape
	Tape is clear
	   you can see beneath it

Color does not offend
   goes with everything
	It is ½-inch wide
	   makes it easy to handle

Made of inexpensive plastic
   practical
   saves the company money
   a modern material
	you do not waste any of it
	It is neatly rolled in a circle
	   tape does not wrinkle

It is small
   you take it anyplace, in
   purse or pocket
	An uncertain amount is left
	on the roll
	   you do not know when it
	   will run out

Disk	**Cutting Edge**

You can pull tape off circle
easily
   you won't waste time
   you won't get angry
	Metal is ½-inch wide
	   metal keeps it from
	   bending
	It has sharp teeth

It is clear plastic
   it is the same as the
   dispenser
	makes the tape easy to tear

of my abstract term, *justice*, might correspond to a quality I had listed under this part of the shirt on my first grid. Asking the question "How is justice like the front of the T-shirt?" I realized that justice must stretch to fit a society, and the members must feel comfortable with it. Looking at my notes about the back of the shirt, I zeroed in on the word *distinguished* and thought aloud how justice must not distinguish among the members of a society on the basis of wealth, race, religion, or sex. Comparing the short sleeves to justice caused me to see justice as the agent in society that allows the members to stay "cool," to stay rational. The double-stitched seams, which gave confidence to the consumer, also gave confidence to a society. The label sewn into the shirt conjured up the image of justice sewn into the fabric of society. My completed grid appears in Table 3.

Table 3

Justice

Front	Label	
It must stretch to fit society People must be comfortable with it It is attractive It makes a society free It makes a statement about a society, person	It is sewn into the fabric of a society It gives a society both a general philosophy and specific laws It enables a society to take proper care of its members It identifies what is harmful to a society It allows people to "breathe," to be themselves	
Back	**Sleeves**	**Seams**
It must be equal for all; must not distinguish on basis of wealth, race, religion, sex It must be practical	It allows for freedom of movement and thoughts It helps people stay rational, keep their cool It keeps society from raveling, falling apart	It creates order It gives confidence, security to people of a society

As we did with my first grid on the parts of the T-shirt, the students and I discussed the qualities of justice on this second grid and how I generated them. We also commented on the strategies I used to overcome frustration, such as seeing words in different contexts, repeating phrases over and over until a thought occurred, thinking of an opposite meaning, or simply pacing the floor.

I ask the students to take their journals home overnight to prepare a grid for their abstract terms based on their written thoughts about their grab-bag objects. I have them complete this stage of the prewriting activity in the privacy of their own living quarters because of the intensity of comparing the abstract term to the concrete object. Writers—students or otherwise—generally require a time period that is not clocked and a place to pace when working through such complex thoughts.

Day 5

Returning with their journals, the students share with the class the qualities they identified concerning their abstract terms. Daniel admitted that he was pleased with the ideas he had generated. He had never examined his thoughts on pride before and now felt confident about his beliefs. While studying his notes on the plastic tape dispenser, he reasoned that pride is often made up of cheap motives which make a person small. The clear roll of tape reminded him that others are able to see beneath our pride, and that one day, like the limited supply of tape, our pride will run out and we will be empty. He equated the center disk with the ease with which we pull out pride to avoid facing problems, and the dispenser's cutting edge demonstrated for him the moral that pride will one day destroy us if we are not careful. Daniel's completed grid appears in Table 4.

After the ideas on the abstract terms are shared, the class and I begin the complex task of organizing these ideas and finding a central focus for an extended definition essay. But the task is easier now because of the wealth of information with which we have to work and the insights we have gained into our own problem-solving abilities. Good writers "discover what they want to do by insistently, energetically exploring the entire problem before them," Flower and Hayes (1980, 31) concluded. Synectic metaphors teach students to broaden their observation and reasoning skills, and to use these cognitive skills to develop strategies for identifying and solving rhetorical problems.

Table 4

Pride

Dispenser	Roll of Tape
It is sometimes made up of cheap reasons for doing something	You can see through it; people can see beneath it
It helps us to save our face	It makes us go in circles; we never get on the straight road
It is sometimes modern; it is not built on old values	One day our pride will run out, and we will be empty
It makes us small	

Disk	Cutting Edge
It can be pulled out easily in any situation	It has an edge which cuts and destroys us
We use it to avoid problems because it is the easy way	It keeps us from bending; we need to bend like the trees to live

References

Flower, Linda, and John R. Hayes. "The Cognition of Discovery: Defining a Rhetorical Problem." *College Composition and Communication* 31, no. 1 (February 1980): 21–32.

———. "A Cognitive Process Theory of Writing." *College Composition and Communication* 32, no. 4 (December 1981): 365–87.

Taylor, Barry P. "Content and Written Form: A Two-Way Street." *TESOL Quarterly* 15, no. 1 (March 1981): 5–13.

Zamel, Vivian. "The Author Responds. . . ." *TESOL Quarterly* 18, no. 1 (March 1984): 154–57.

Whose Territory? Watch It!

Derise J. Wigand
Washington State University, Pullman

Kathleen Smith-Meadows
Washington State University, Pullman

This writing project originated with our attempt to devise an appropriate assignment for developing the thinking and writing skills of students in the sciences and social sciences. At Washington State University, students in many of these majors are now required by their departments to take a senior/graduate-level class in "Professional and Technical Writing," but clearly they need such skills in their sophomore and junior classwork and need more than raw beginners' skills in the senior-level class. Thus inspired, we developed this writing project for freshman composition classes at WSU. The entire project involves three papers—a summary, a proposal, and a report.

The Project—Begin with Reading

The writing project centers around an article called "Territorial Behaviour," excerpted from Desmond Morris's book *Manwatching: A Field Guide to Human Behaviour*. This article is a lively, readable piece (about 4,000 words long) explaining that territorial behavior, a characteristic usually attributed to animals, is also exhibited by humans. Although the ideas Morris explains and illustrates with many vivid examples would seem to be common knowledge, students often comment that they never noticed or understood these behaviors before. The article provides a theory and various subordinate hypotheses for students to test. It has the advantage that eighteen and nineteen year olds are interested in human behavior and have developed some expertise, however subconscious, in deciphering and responding to it. Using this article for the project also has the advantage that human behavior is easy to observe in everyday life and doesn't require a fancy microscope in the classroom or extensive science and math backgrounds for non-science majors, yet students deal with scientific generalizations to explain observable events.

Objective Summary

Stage one of the writing project involves writing an objective summary of Morris's article within a strict word limit. Brief abstracts are commonly required for articles submitted to journals, but this important skill is not often practiced by students. "Territorial Behaviour" is complex enough and loaded with enough details and examples to make this first paper a challenge. Many students are misled by the simple opening lines: "A territory is a defended space. In the broadest sense, there are three kinds of human territory: tribal, family and personal." But Morris's ideas go beyond this simple definition and classification, as thinking students soon realize. As a preliminary step, students can be asked to read the article and prepare a two-sentence summary (no word limit but *only* two sentences). They bring these minisummaries to class, where half a dozen students are selected at random to write their summaries on the board during class discussion of the article.

Next students are assigned to write a formal summary (i.e., for a grade) in no more than 500 words (about two pages). They are instructed to pick out the most important ideas from the many minor ideas and to decide whether or not to include examples (their own or Morris's) that illustrate the ideas and how many examples to include. The summarization assignment also provides an opportunity to discuss plagiarism and to demonstrate the techniques of excerpting and punctuating quotations. In observing a word limit, students are pressured to concentrate more ideas in fewer words and sentences and to step beyond merely repeating Morris's organizational pattern.

As they go over the rough drafts in editing groups, students may complain about the boredom of reading the same ideas over and over, but they do see how other writers handled the task and may spot holes in the ideas they presented in their own summaries. By first reading and discussing, then drafting, and then reviewing their work after a session with editing groups, student writers have numerous opportunities to examine their ideas and their writing style in the early stages of composing the paper—the process followed for each of the three parts of this project. These summaries are fairly quick for instructors to grade, and they indicate how well the students understand the article before they progress to the research stages of the project.

Research Proposal

Researchers commonly use or extend another researcher's ideas or theories, and they devise experiments to confirm those ideas or to extend knowledge of the details. This project begins similarly. The students have read and summarized Morris's ideas and now are assigned to devise experiments to test those ideas; they are to discover their own additions to the examples and details that show how territorial behavior works in real life with real people.

We have students form groups of three to five members who will together devise and run such experiments. They pool their data, but each student is required to write his or her own proposal (about two to four pages) and report (five to ten pages). Students spend one or two class periods in their groups planning (with the instructor circulating and advising them) and then run their experiments outside of class—in elevators or the library or wherever they decide.

Since our students usually live on campus, personal territory is the type of territory most practical for experimentation; however, high school students could also do research involving family territory. Morris mentions one experiment in his article: "Experiments in a library revealed that placing a pile of magazines on the table in one seating position successfully reserved that place for an average of 77 minutes. If a sports-jacket was added, draped over the chair, then the 'reservation effect' lasted for two hours." Although some students have tried this, most quickly think of their own unique hypothesis to try. For those few who are still uninspired, we also outline experiments that our previous students have devised—observing arrangements of people riding in elevators; noting the "reservation effects" of grocery carts in stores or of coats, books, and quarters on video games; observing speaking distances between men or women in varying situations; invading personal space in the student union or dorm TV room.

In devising their experiments, the student groups commonly stumble into several lapses of logic in their research. They usually have too many ideas and attempt to prove too much for the limited scope of the assigned papers. For example, a group may decide to observe the distances at which people walk, stand, and sit from each other and propose to have each group member observe students in dining halls, the student union, the bus, and the gyms for a month. They may hypothesize that two women acquaintances will sit closer than two men, that a boyfriend and girlfriend will sit closer than the two women, and that a husband and wife will sit even closer; they may further hypothesize that when these same people are walking, the space between them may increase or decrease. Such an experiment, as the instructor can point out, must be narrowed dramatically to focus on some small part of these ideas—in this example, perhaps just observing students in the dining hall when a stranger sits by them. Without such narrowing, the experiment will be poorly controlled and difficult for any other researcher to replicate, another important factor in experimentation.

Another pitfall with a too broad experiment is that students cannot monitor enough similar cases to provide sufficient evidence to verify their hypotheses. Here the students quickly realize the ultimate limitations of time and money for carrying out their research. Ideally, they would test the entire population of the university riding on the city bus, but of course they cannot—no scientist can. But how many cases are enough? A dozen? A hundred? A thousand? Students sometimes submit reports testing only three subjects sitting in the student union—two women and a man—and then wonder why their instructor disputes their claims that men are more hostile to invaders of their space. Certainly, students do not have enough time to sample a thousand cases, as professional researchers would, but the group members must decide on reasonable numbers of cases to test—for example, testing thirty subjects sitting in the student union in order to support their claims. They must also consider what factors (such as sex, race, age) will affect their results and must design their experiment to control for such variables—for example, testing fifteen women and fifteen men, all Americans of undergraduate age.

Some of these pitfalls in design can be avoided by having students read sample proposals from previous classes. (If this project is assigned for the first time, groups can present their experimental designs to the whole class for discussion and evaluation. Alternatively, the instructor could create models.[1]) We spend one class period discussing these sample proposals, looking for pitfalls: Does the experiment really test the proposed hypothesis? Is the procedure clearly explained? Do the researchers control the experiment carefully—not trying to test too much? Do they test enough cases to "prove" anything? Can any hypothesis *ever* be "proven"? Is it hazardous? (The latter question is worth mentioning because some students have taken risks doing space invasion experiments. One student purposely squeezed between a man and woman riding an elevator together—he received verbal abuse and certainly risked a punch, too. Luckily, most students are so attuned to spatial rules, as Morris says, that they don't want to try such aggressive experiments.) In discussing both the previous experiments and the students' own proposals, it is up to the instructor to push, prod, and even temporarily confuse the students' thinking processes so that students grapple with the logic of their proposed experimentation.

Reading and discussing the sample proposals also demonstrates to students the "standard" format for their proposals: background (outline of Morris), hypothesis (extending Morris's ideas to anticipate what should happen in their experiment), and procedure (where, how, how many, etc.). Instructors can choose or create one model that is conspicuously skimpy in detail and present others that show good use of details as well as subheadings and diagrams. Evaluating these models in class usually stimulates better planning and writing and fewer pitfalls than any amount of lecturing by the instructor.

The last step in this stage of the project, before running the experiments, is for students to meet and share their written proposals in editing sessions with other members of each student's group and with members of other groups—in the same way that scientists submit their proposals to outside reviewers. These student editors and the instructor can guide the student researchers to think and write clearly about their research and to avoid the pitfalls before they move on to the next stages. Students hand in their revised proposals and then carry out their experiments. Afterward, they spend one class period discussing their data and their results before they tackle the reports.

Final Report

At some point while the experiments are being run, the class can again read and discuss copies of several sample reports, both good and bad, from previous students. Again, the students see some of the lapses in logic that their peers fell into or avoided and again see models of the "standard" format they should follow: background/hypothesis, procedure, results, and discussion/conclusions. Clearly, the first two parts can be largely taken from their original proposals, though revisions are usually required after the actual experiments are run. As we evaluate the sample proposals in class, we discuss the questions raised earlier and talk about some new ones: Are the results clearly summarized? Are charts and diagrams appropriate and properly labeled? Do the results justify the conclusions? What further experiments or modifications of this experiment are suggested by the results? These are the classic questions of scientific inquiry, yet most students have had little experience with this type of writing or even this kind of thinking. Few have thought about what kind of graphs are appropriate, as is evidenced when their own reports come in with line graphs connecting random events or with bar graphs lacking labels. Few have employed subheadings to help organize a longer expository paper.

Several more pitfalls often become evident when students reach the editing stages of their reports. If the teacher anticipates these problems and provides an editing guide (a quick checklist of common problems), many of these pitfalls can be uncovered when students bring the rough drafts of their papers to class for their peers to read. Readers from each student's own research group and from other groups should read the papers and add critical comments. Sometimes the comments reveal that students have focused their attention on their own actions rather than on their subjects' reactions. As Morris notes, we know that a dog marks territory by urination, not because it urinates around the yard, but because other dogs respect these markers if the territory holder is in the yard. Students must also shift their focus to the subjects they observed. They must also be thorough in their presentation of results and conclusions. In the conclusion section of one report, the student merely noted that he and his partner "went in the student lounge afterwards and discussed the results," but he failed to realize that he should report their conclusions to the reader. Often students fail to maintain an objective voice about personal experiences ("Bingo, I thought, did he ever work well into the experiment!"). Another common problem with the final report is that the students collect more information than they can account for, so often their accounts are not as linear nor discussions as succinct as those by a more accomplished writer. Or students mistakenly put information under the wrong subheadings.

One variation of the project that we have used is to have the members of each group work together to prepare and present the proposal and final report orally to the whole class. Unfortunately, the proposals are often rather dry and do not elicit many helpful comments from the class. However, the final reports are excellent, fueled by the enthusiastic anecdotes of real-life research (usually detailing how the procedure went wrong when a subject did something unexpected), and spark many interested questions from classmates. One group even brought in a video cassette recorder to show a videotape of its experiment with subjects' responses to a poll. Oral presentations add one more skill to a complex range of skills covered in the project.

Overall Assessment

All in all, we find that this project leads to a successful writing experience for our students. They perceive the assignment as practical and useful for their futures. It brings their expert, if previously subconscious, knowledge of human behavior to bear on the topic and improves their skills in examining their own thinking and writing, along with that of their peers, through the use of model papers and editing groups during the stages of the writing process. To successfully complete the entire assignment, students must use three modes of thought—reflection, analysis, and argumentation. The project combines the traditional approach of writing about reading with more experiential heuristics. Though this project involves "scientific" experimentation, English teachers have the training and experience with rhetorical logic to understand and anticipate the major pitfalls that a student will face.

That this writing project teaches students to think and engages them in the writing process is shown by the large number (up to two-thirds of a class) who choose to rewrite their reports at the end of the semester for another grade. These rewritten papers are clearly superior to the first efforts in that the hypotheses and discussions more completely and clearly account for the data. Obviously, the students continue to contemplate Morris's ideas and their experiments for some time. As one student remarked, Morris's ideas on territorial behavior are so simple, but he never thought about them before. Now he can't help but smile as he notices where his fellow riders stand in an elevator.

Note

1. The authors are willing to share a few model papers with interested teachers. Send a stamped, self-addressed envelope to the authors in care of the Department of English, Washington State University, Pullman, WA 83702.

Reference

Morris, Desmond. *Manwatching: A Field Guide to Human Behavior.* New York: Harry N. Abrams, 1977. Available in Randall E. Decker, ed., *Patterns of Exposition* 7 (1980), 8 (1982), and 9 (n.d.). Boston: Little, Brown.

The Sentence:
A Tool for Teaching
Straight Thinking

Walter F. Utroske
Eastern Montana College, Billings

A good many approaches to teaching straight thinking through writing seem to involve fairly long units of discourse—the paragraph, the essay, the research paper. This emphasis on extended discourse is understandable in that full-blown argumentation, analysis, synthesis, and evaluation are processes which need to unfold and which require extended development. Nevertheless, students also can make significant strides in learning critical thinking skills through a much shorter and more manageable unit of discourse: the sentence. Here I speak not of the isolated dummy sentence, but of the sentence which, as James Moffett and Betty Jane Wagner explain, is a complete discourse by virtue of its conveying a purposeful message from writer to reader (Moffett and Wagner 1983, 8–13, 365–70). As long as a sentence is this kind of a whole unto itself, it is an effective instructional unit, and teachers at all levels can use it as one tool for teaching straight thinking.

Five classroom activities which I have adapted from Vincent Ruggiero, Ludwig Wittgenstein, George Barr, and, primarily, Moffett and Wagner can activate students' thinking. The sequence of activities outlined below is designed to move students from concrete, low-level thinking toward abstract, high-level thinking as espoused by Benjamin Bloom in his taxonomy of educational objectives. Directions are given in abbreviated fashion; teachers can adjust the procedure and content of each activity to accommodate their students' abilities. At all times, though, students must strive to write sentences which are complete discourses—a writer's purposeful message to a reader—rather than isolated "exercise" sentences with no context.

You See What?

In an activity that helps students recognize alternative perspectives,[1] the instructor uses an overhead projector to display the illustrations shown in Figures 1, 2, and 3. Each illustration appears for fifteen

Figure 1. Duck-rabbit (Wittgenstein 1970, 194).

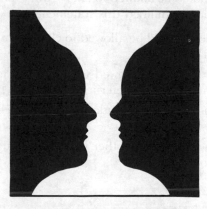

Figure 2. Vase and two faces (Ruggiero 1984, 214).

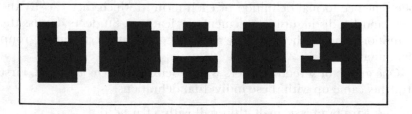

Figure 3. Hidden word (Barr 1968, 120).

seconds; then students write one-sentence explanations of what they see in the illustration. The class debates, discusses, and revises the explanations, and students usually reach a consensus about the possible ways of perceiving each illustration.

Refining Dichotomous Thinking

This activity helps students learn to detect dichotomous thinking and to qualify and refine these thoughts.[2] Working individually or in groups, students examine one-sentence yes-or-no statements. When they are familiar with the mutually exclusive nature of these statements, they write their own one-sentence dichotomous statements and follow cues (such as *when?* or *why?*) to prepare qualified statements.

For example, one class wrote the following dichotomous statement: "We sixth graders should be allowed to chew gum." Through classroom discussion, the students qualified this statement:

> We sixth graders should be allowed to chew gum whenever we are doing seat work. *(When?)*
>
> Sixth graders should be allowed to chew gum in the library, the halls, the bathroom, the cafeteria, and outside. *(Where?)*
>
> Chewing gum lets us sixth graders relax and helps us think while we study. *(Why?)*
>
> Chewing gum in class can bother your friends just like whispering and talking do. *(Why not?)*

Writing Formal Definitions

As students write one-sentence definitions, they classify pertinent information and ideas about a term (either a concrete object or an abstract concept). Students meet in small groups to discuss possible definitions of three to five terms. Then students work independently to write a one-sentence formal definition of each term in which they classify the term and list distinguishing elements or features. Students discuss the definitions within their groups and by consensus arrive at a group definition.

One group of seventh graders was to define the term *wire brad*. First students came up with these individual definitions:

> A wire brad is a small, thin nail with a flat head.

A wire brad is a skinny tack used for light carpentry work.

A wire brad is about an inch-long nail with a flat head and a thin shaft.

The group discussed the individual definitions and incorporated elements of each in the consensus definition: "A wire brad is a thin, flat-headed metal nail between a half inch and one inch long, which is used to secure light wood joints or to attach small accessories to wood."

Writing Aphorisms

By writing aphorisms, students learn to perceive the relationship between the specific and the general and learn to qualify such statements.[3] Students listen to an aphorism or adage, and then each student, in one sentence, interprets, supports, or refutes the aphorism according to his or her experience. For example, the aphorism "He who hesitates is lost" was interpreted by one student to mean "If you react to situations too deliberately, you will often find yourself at a disadvantage."

Next students write their own aphorisms and a one-sentence supporting statement. These are read aloud, and classmates suggest revision. One third grader's aphorism, "Brothers and sisters are natural enemies," was supported with the statement "All the brothers and sisters I know of at school and at Sunday school are always fighting with each other."

Making Value Judgments

This activity has students exercise the progressively complex thought processes of listing, comparing, and evaluation.[4] Students begin by describing three pleasant personal experiences. For example, one eighth grader wrote the following:

Last weekend my dad and I went skiing.

I enjoyed the picnic at Foster's house Wednesday evening.

Helping serve soup at the rescue mission on Easter morning made me feel good.

Next students write a one-sentence comparative or contrastive statement about two of the items on the first list. The student above wrote, "Helping serve soup at the rescue mission gave me a better feeling than attending Foster's picnic did." Students then write a one-sentence value judgment about each item on the first list. The eighth grader wrote the following:

> Going on a weekend skiing trip with your dad is an excellent way to keep the lines of communication open between you and him.
>
> The food at Foster's picnic was good, but the punch tasted awful.
>
> Working at the rescue mission is the most Christian act one can do at Easter time.

Notes

1. See Ruggiero (1984, 96–103) for a detailed discussion of alternative perspectives.

2. This activity is adapted from Moffett and Wagner (1983, 94).

3. See Moffett and Wagner (1983, 367–68) for a variation of this activity and for other suggestions about aphorisms.

4. See Moffett and Wagner (1983, 378) for a variation of this activity.

References

Barr, George. *Fun and Tricks for Young Scientists.* New York: McGraw-Hill, 1968.

Moffett, James, and Betty Jane Wagner. *Student-Centered Language Arts and Reading, K–13: A Handbook for Teachers.* 3d ed. Boston: Houghton Mifflin, 1983.

Ruggiero, Vincent Ryan. *The Art of Thinking: A Guide to Critical and Creative Thought.* New York: Harper and Row, 1984.

Wittgenstein, Ludwig. *Philosophical Investigations.* 3d ed. Translated by G.E.M. Anscombe. New York: Macmillan, 1970.

From "Thinking Man" to "Man Thinking": Exercises Requiring Problem-Solving Skills

Deborah J. Barrett
Houston Baptist University, Houston, Texas

Educators would certainly agree with substituting the word *students* for *man* in Sir Joshua Reynolds's statement that "there is no expedient to which a man will not resort to avoid the real labor of thinking." Making students think—really think, instead of imitating or simply repeating information—is never easy, but with well-chosen exercises, it is possible to encourage the labor of thinking. For my freshman composition classes, I have designed four exercises that require students to concentrate and to use reasoning. In order to succeed in the assignments, students must use their heads; there is no easy answer or easy way out. I present the exercises as progressive, starting with basic reasoning and moving to much more complex reasoning and use of the imagination, but each unit could be used independently. The assignments range from the mundane to the sublime: the first requires students to punctuate difficult passages in order to make sense out of them; the second asks students to read closely and to use basic reasoning to solve short mysteries; the third calls for students to write an argument based upon close reading and problem solving; and the fourth allows students to use their imaginations to create the ending for an unfinished story by Mark Twain.

Assignment I: Making Sense out of Apparent Nonsense

In the first set of exercises, the students are given passages without punctuation and are asked to punctuate the sentences so that they make sense. Henry James and Shakespeare are particularly rich sources of complicated sentences, but nearly any complex sentence will work. Since the first two passages are real brainteasers, it is best to do them in class, allowing a set amount of time (thirty minutes will usually do), so that the teacher can judge the students' level of frustration and offer encouragement. Students often declare that they see no way to make sense of the sentences, but if you guarantee that they do make sense and that each student possesses the knowledge of punctuation needed to make sense of them, students will plod on. The result usually surprises students. They learn that they really do know more about punctuation than they will usually admit, and they also learn the importance of, as well as the reason behind, our sometimes bewildering little marks of punctuation. I hand out the following quotations to the students and later display the answer key with the overhead projector.

The Importance of the Mundane; or,
"I never knew a comma could mean so much"

Punctuate the following passages so that they make sense. Examples *A*, *B*, and *C* are more than one sentence; thus, you will need to add internal marks (commas, semicolons, colons, dashes) as well as end marks (periods, question marks, or exclamation marks) and appropriate capitalization. Example *D* is only one sentence; thus, only internal marks are needed. Also, in *B* and *D* you may need to add internal quotation marks.

A.   That that is is that that is not is not that that is not is not that that is that that is is not that that is not is not that it it is. (Ravenel 1959, 143)

B.   John while James had had had had had had had had had had had a better effect on the teacher. (Fixx 1972, 29)

C.   Why if thou never wast [were] at court thou never sawest [saw] good manners if thou never sawest good manners then thy manners must be wicked and wickedness is sin and sin is damnation thou are in a parlous state shepherd. (William Shakespeare, *As You Like It*, Act 3, Scene 2, lines 40–44)

D.   He had come putting the thing pompously to look at his property which he had thus for a third of a century not been within four thousand miles of or expressing it less sordidly he had yielded to the humour of seeing again his house on the jolly corner as he usually and quite fondly described it the one in which he had first seen the light in which various members of his family had lived and had died in which the holidays of his overschooled boyhood had been passed and the few social flowers of his chilled adolescence gathered and which alienated then for so long a period had through the successive deaths of his two brothers and the termination of old arrangements come wholly into his hands. (Henry James, "The Jolly Corner," in James 1965, 194–95)

Answer Key for "The Importance of the Mundane"

A.   That, that is, is. That, that is not, is not. That, that is not, is
     not that that is. That, that is, is not that, that is not. Is not
     that it? It is.

B.   John, while James had had "had," had had "had had." "Had
     had" had had a better effect on the teacher.

C.   Why, if thou never wast at court, thou never sawest good
     manners; if thou never sawest good manners, then thy
     manners must be wicked; and wickedness is sin, and sin is
     damnation. Thou art in a parlous state, shepherd.

D.   He had come—putting the thing pompously—to look at his
     "property," which he had thus for a third of a century not
     been within four thousand miles of; or, expressing it less
     sordidly, he had yielded to the humour of seeing again his
     house on the jolly corner as he usually, and quite fondly,
     described it—the one in which he had first seen the light, in
     which various members of his family had lived and had died,
     in which the holidays of his overschooled boyhood had been
     passed and the few social flowers of his chilled adolescence
     gathered, and which, alienated then for so long a period,
     had, through the successive deaths of his two brothers and
     the termination of old arrangements, come wholly into his
     hands.

It is important to allow time to discuss how the students decided on
which punctuation mark to use and where to place it. What emerges
from the discussion is the students' realization that they do know
something about "correct" or, more accurately, "effective" punctuation
and about the positions of subjects, verbs, and objects. When I produce
the answer key, I point out that although the marks in examples *C* and
D are the ones used by Shakespeare and James or their editors, other
marks would work as well. The point is to make the passage make sense
to the average reader, and whatever marks accomplish that are perfectly
acceptable.

Assignment II: Solving the Mystery

For many students, this unit is the most fun. Students are given a
ratiocinative tale with the solution omitted and are asked to supply the
solution. Any standard mystery writer would probably do; the key is to
keep the selection short (no more than ten pages). I use selections from

Eric R. Emmet's *Brain Puzzler's Delight* or from Donald Sobol's Encyclopedia Brown series of mysteries for young readers. Whether I use
Emmet or Sobol depends upon the makeup of my class. Really sharp
students or perhaps those who are quite "serious" or "sophisticated"
may be insulted by mystery stories designed for young people.

The Emmet selections require much more time and effort than the
Sobol mysteries, but they certainly teach the fundamentals of reading
carefully, concentrating on a problem, and mapping out ideas in some
ordered way. Two of the best selections for classroom use are "Who
Killed Popoff?" and "The Poison Spreads." To solve "Popoff," the
students are required to establish syllogisms and to determine which
statements are false and which are true. "Poison" requires diagrams
and grids or some kind of chart to separate and organize the
information.

The Encyclopedia Brown mysteries are much less elaborate, but they,
too, require close reading and close attention to details. They are much
less likely to frustrate the slower student. Solving the mystery usually
depends upon recognizing some mistake in the culprit's version of how
something happened. For instance, in "The Case of the Two-Dollar
Bill," the crook claims to have placed the stolen two-dollar bill between
pages 157 and 158 of a gray book, which would be impossible since
these would always be the recto and verso sides of the same page. In
"The Case of Bugs's Kidnapping," the supposedly kidnapped Bugs
says that he could have escaped, but the door hinges were on the other
side of the door; when Bugs claims to have been knocked down by the
same door as the supposed kidnapper came into the room, Encyclopedia Brown recognizes that Bugs must be lying since doors open
toward their hinges.

I give the students the passage with brief instructions, a time limit
of thirty minutes or so, and a heading such as "Who did it? Or do you
really expect me to figure this out?" Few of the students can solve the
mystery in the time limit, but the purpose of the exercise is to discern
the method of solution as much as to find the solution. If, however, the
students insist on solving the whole puzzle on their own, I let them take
the passage home and give them the solution at the next class meeting.

Assignment III: Writing an Argumentative Essay

This assignment centers upon Faulkner's "A Rose for Emily" and
concludes with students writing an argumentative essay on this short
story. Students must read the story very carefully, paying close attention
to details and using their ratiocinative skills from the previous exercise

to complete a chronology of the events in Emily's life. Since even Faulkner scholars argue about the exact dates in the story,[1] we cannot expect our students to come up with a definitive answer; however, I have found that some of my students have established very sound arguments for their chronologies.

After students have read the story and we have discussed it in class, I give them the following handout:

Another Mystery—Why Did Emily Kill Homer?

On the chart provided below, fill in the requested information. Obviously, "A Rose for Emily" is not told in chronological order, but Faulkner gives you numerous clues as to the important events in Emily Grierson's life. Your first task is to figure out the chronological order of the events which reveal Emily's upbringing and patterns of action. Once you have decided upon the important dates, fill in the chart below. Unless you are a master sleuth or genius, you will need to work on scratch paper until you have the chronology set.

Date	Age	Section	Event	Significance

The chart that I give to students covers the rest of the handout page. I require that they use the chart so that all students present the information in the same form.

I allot forty-five minutes in class for the students to work on the assignment and then ask them to finish it at home, warning that they are to do their own work. I stress to students that they should do their best and that they should pay close attention to each detail as they determine the chronology of events in Emily's life.

At the next class meeting, we go over the chronology, and I ask a few students to explain how they decided upon the dates of events. After about thirty minutes, I give the students the second part of the assignment:

Why Did Emily Kill Homer?—Part II

Now that you have a chronology of the important events in Emily's life, you know a lot about her. Write an argumentative essay explaining why you think Emily killed Homer. If you want to argue that Emily is insane, you must present evidence. It is not sufficient simply to say, "Emily killed Homer because she is crazy; anyone who would do what she did would have to be." Think of yourself as an attorney attempting to convince a jury that your client is insane. Use the events that you isolated to support your argument.

If you do not have enough to think about, here is a quotation from Robert Browning's poem "Porphyria's Lover," in which you might see some similarity to Emily's action. If you do not see any relationship, just take it as another of my attempts to broaden your horizons and go read the rest of the poem in your "spare" time.

> at last I knew
> Porphyria worshipped me: surprise
> Made my heart swell, and still it grew
> While I debated what to do.
> That moment she was mine, mine, fair,
> Perfectly pure and good: I found
> A thing to do, and all her hair
> In one long yellow string I wound
> Three times her little throat around,
> And strangled her.

So much for edification. Your essay is due one week from today. Turn in your chronology and a brief explanation of how you sorted out the dates with your paper.

Assignment IV—Creating an Ending

In this final assignment, the students should be able to use all of the skills practiced in the previous exercises and have fun. First, I have them read Mark Twain's "A Medieval Romance," a spoof of medieval romances with an elaborate, progressively entangling plot. Twain ends the tale as follows:

> The remainder of this thrilling and eventful story will NOT be found in this or any other publication, either now or at any future time.
> The truth is, I have got my hero (or heroine) into such a particularly close place that I do not see how I am ever going to get him (or her) out of it again, and therefore I will wash my hands of the whole business, and leave that person to get out the best way that offers—or else stay there. I thought it was going to be easy enough to straighten out that little difficulty, but it looks different now. (232)

After the students have read the story, I hand out the following assignment:

You Mean That I Get to Be Twain for a Day?

Reread "A Medieval Romance" very carefully, noting the relationships of the characters and their motives, and also paying careful
attention to Twain's tone. Now, write an ending for the story.
Attempt to capture Twain's tone and be sure that your conclusion
follows logically from the rest of the story. Let your imaginations
go. Is there a way to get the characters out of their predicament
to produce the happy ending that such a story dictates? How
might that be accomplished? Assume Twain's persona and pretend
that you have decided to go back and write an ending for his
unfinished tale, for as Aristotle emphasized, we must have a
"completed action."

I first tried this assignment with high school students and was
surprised at how well they did. My college students have also done well,
amazing themselves with their own creativity and often feeling rather
smug that they solved a problem that Twain claimed to have found
insolvable.

The goal of all of the assignments is to move the students beyond
what Emerson labeled "thinking man" to the higher level of "man
thinking," that is, to have students actively engaged in using their
minds. The assignments force students to read closely, approach a
problem from their existing knowledge, and work at the problem until
they solve it or at least until they work out a plan for solving it. Just
knowing how to attack a problem demonstrates reasoning ability and
is an important skill. By the end of the semester, the students should
recognize that problem-solving skills can be applied to something as
mundane as how to punctuate a sentence and as sublime as creating
their own fiction. They certainly learn that "real" thinking is labor and
that nothing will take its place.

Note

1. Although my own chronology does not agree with that proposed by
Cleanth Brooks (1978, 382–84), his discussion of problems encountered by
chronologies that place Emily's death in the 1930s and his presentation of his
own chronology warrant attention by anyone working with the story.

References

Brooks, Cleanth. *William Faulkner: Toward Yoknapatawpha and Beyond.* New
Haven, Conn.: Yale University Press, 1978.

Emmet, Eric R. *Brain Puzzler's Delight*. Hillside, N.J.: Enslow Publications, 1978.

Fixx, James F. *Games for the Super-Intelligent*. Garden City, N.Y.: Doubleday, 1972.

James, Henry. "The Jolly Corner." In *The Complete Tales of Henry James*, vol. 12, edited by Leon Edel. Philadelphia: J. B. Lippincott, 1965.

Ravenel, William B. *English Reference Book*. Alexandria, Va.: Virginia Publishers, 1959.

Twain, Mark. "A Medieval Romance." In *Sketches: New and Old*. St. Clair Shores, Mich.: Scholarly Press, 1981.

Protocol Analysis for the Student Writer

Gyde Christine Martin
Texas Christian University, Fort Worth

In his essay "Teaching the Other Self: The Writer's First Reader," Donald Murray (1982) describes the kind of critical thinking which goes on during the act of writing

> as a conversation between two workmen muttering to each other at the workbench. The self speaks, the other self listens and responds. The self proposes, the other self considers. The self makes, the other self evaluates. The two selves collaborate: a problem is spotted, discussed, defined; solutions are proposed, rejected, suggested, attempted, tested, discarded, accepted. (165)

In the teaching of writing to college freshmen, we constantly try to stimulate this kind of inner dialogue with a variety of methods. We write questions on the margins of student papers to challenge students to rethink; in conferences we try to engage them in critical discussions over their papers; and some of us may even employ computers to engage the searching writer in a dialogue with a simulated interlocutor whose questions are designed to lead the writer to a closer definition of his or her topic. All these methods, however, have one thing in common: they try to stimulate a dialogue within one student's mind by simulating this internal discussion with an external dialogue between two minds. We hope that the student writer will somehow internalize this external dialogue and will learn to raise and consider these critical questions.

Murray suggests that rather than acting as the second "workman" and thus doing a crucial part of the work for the student, writing teachers should have faith in students' capacity to think critically and should use the conference to listen as students criticize their own writing and thus instruct themselves to make changes. This kind of conference is intended to give writers confidence in their ability to recognize and solve problems, so that they become more independent of their critical advisor. The teacher should ask questions only if students have nothing to say about their own writing, and then only questions about the

47

writing process, questions which cause students to remember the conscious decisions they made based on independent critical thinking.

Murray's conferences are designed to nurture writers' capacity for critical thinking, but they do not seem to allow for intervention if students are making "unwise" decisions about their writing or if their critical thinking is illogical. What I am proposing is a way of using protocol analysis, not as a research method but as a teaching method which, like Murray's conferences, makes writers aware of their critical capacity and which also allows students to trace and analyze *how* they think and compose.

A Log of Questions Encountered during Writing

Since writing obliterates most of its own traces, we can usually follow the growth of a text only through the succession of its drafts. Yet all the drafts reveal are the solutions to problems, the answers to questions that were raised before the drafting or redrafting. To obtain a more complete record, I asked students in my writing workshop and some of my colleagues to keep a running account of the problems—substantive, rhetorical, or editorial—which they encountered in the course of composing. I also kept an account. To facilitate notation, these problems were recorded in question form. Since drafting involves changing, I also asked these writers to reconstruct the questions and concerns that arose during the drafting, whether or not the writers acted on them. Although these reconstructed protocols cannot provide a record of the composing process in the manner of Flower and Hayes's tape-recorded protocols, they do reflect writers' conscious choices, the logic underlying their decisions, and many of their false starts.

This composing record is actually a map of a writer's journey toward the final draft, consisting of a question log which records the writer's effort to define the writing task (depending on the task, this may involve identifying one's audience, finding the subject, the topic, an angle, an approach, etc.), the first draft with its preliminary answers and solutions, a reconstructed log of the. questions that arose during the drafting, and in some cases more logs which record subsequent revisions. In other words, the writer is holding in hand the tangible evidence of his or her critical thinking, of the many inner dialogues that resulted in the production of the text.

A Log of Questions Encountered Prior to Writing

Being aware of one's capacity to think critically, however, is not enough. Student writers can benefit also from knowing how they think and compose and from reviewing and evaluating their own strategies. The record left in the form of question logs and drafts gives the students and instructor the opportunity to "diagnose" these strategies.

The task that I assigned to my students was to examine a list of some three hundred bumper sticker slogans, which they had helped to collect over several weeks, and to make observations about bumper stickers as a social phenomenon. In response, Carol generated a list of twenty-four questions, which began with these six:

1. What am I going to write about?
2. Do the bumper stickers compare?
3. Do they contrast?
4. Should I write my paper on comparison/contrast?
5. Or why people put bumper stickers on their cars?
6. Are people serious when they put a particular sticker on their car?

Carol's first concern was with the content of her future paper, but immediately she became preoccupied with its form and structure. She was envisioning a paper in the comparison and contrast mode without yet knowing what to compare or for which purpose. Then Carol must have sensed that this approach was a dead end, for in her fifth question she turned to the material, the bumper sticker slogans, and proposed enquiring into people's motives for displaying bumper stickers. In her following nine questions Carol explored several other related avenues—why some people do not display bumper stickers on their cars; whether she herself would put one on her car; if so, which one and why—but in question sixteen she returned to her earlier concern with motives and continued to explore along this line:

17. Where do I start?
18. Are there different groups of bumper stickers?
19. Do different groups of people put the same bumper stickers on their cars?
20. What are the different groups?

This line of enquiry shows that Carol was trying to bring order to the material by categorizing bumper stickers according to the types of people who display them. In her first draft of the paper these "types of people" were identified as those who are "proud" (of their native state, bar, school, hobby, job, etc.), those who are "angry" (at Yankees, at antiabortionists, at tailgaters, etc.), and those who have "a good sense of humor" because their bumper stickers are just meant to make one laugh.

To enable Carol to learn from her own protocol, at this stage the teacher needs to point out Carol's successful decisions: to abandon the mode approach and to continue her search for a viable approach. To know what she has done will give Carol confidence in her decisions and intuitions. However, the log can also indicate her deficiencies, in this case Carol's decision to classify the people rather than the bumper stickers, which led her inevitably into stereotyping on the basis of inferences. The instructor can show Carol where her critical thinking went awry, where her inner dialogue broke off and she simply accepted this way of classifying without challenging it. The role of the teacher during this diagnosis is not to point out alternatives or to offer ready-made solutions, but to reengage the writer in that inner dialogue in which his or her own solutions are "proposed, rejected, suggested, attempted, tested, discarded, accepted."

Carol's question log is not the only one to reveal such preoccupation with form. Christine, although not envisioning a final product in a certain mode, seemed to approach the task with a rigid strategy of what is important in a paper:

1. What effect would I get if I opened my paper discussing bumper stickers in general and all the different kinds, giving examples?
2. Would this be too broad? Should I be more specific?
3. Maybe this would be too boring to the reader?
4. What type of audience would I write for?
5. Should I try to be broad enough for a variety of readers or should I get specific and center my paper on a specific group of people?
6. What about taking a specific type of bumper stickers like the "I ♡ . . ." stickers and developing a paper from those?
7. Would that give me enough to write about?
8. What about writing about the purpose of bumper stickers?
9. Would this be interesting?
10. Where could I find information?

Christine seemed to be working from a checklist of "rules about good writing." She had learned that the opening paragraph is crucial in captivating the reader's attention, that moving from the general to the specific is an acceptable structure for the paragraph, that there is danger in being too general in one's treatment of the topic, and that one should tailor the topic to the audience. Like Carol, Christine was worrying about how to present her observations before she had even made any, but unlike Carol, she continued this dead-end approach until she became frustrated and demanded a clearer definition of the assignment. Since Christine needed to unlearn those rules about good writing, at this point the instructor should "unteach" Christine by using the log to show her exactly what she has been doing, i.e., worrying unnecessarily about questions that may become relevant once she begins to write and maybe not even then. And for encouragement, Christine also needs to learn that she has touched on something much more relevant in questions six and eight, and that she should continue to examine the material and rely on her own observations because she probably would not find any information about bumper stickers in outside sources.

Since Christine's question log revealed that she had once learned some hints for analyzing or revising, I was curious to see what her revised drafts and their corresponding question logs would look like. The question log prepared after her first draft of the paper contained only four questions, three that proposed including more examples of bumper stickers and one that asked about the appropriateness of beginning with a rhetorical question. The third question log recorded the changes made as Christine wrote her second draft. In it she debated whether to adopt that rhetorical question as her title and to repeat the question at the end as a concluding sentence. But apart from these two questions involving sentences, Christine's major concerns were editorial: spelling, punctuation, and frequent stylistic changes on the word or phrase level. Most of the students' revision logs showed that they understood revising as editing, which supports the observations by Nancy Sommers (1980, 383) and by Lester Faigley and Stephen Witte that inexperienced writers "tend to revise locally, ignoring the situational constraints" (1981, 411).

To encourage one more attempt at revision, we sometimes have students rewrite their papers from a different point of view (perhaps as seen with the eyes of a Martian) or for a different audience, but these changes affect the situational constraints and create a different writing task. Instead, the writer needs to learn to interact once more with the task and the text at hand and needs to learn to experiment. To encourage global revision, the question log can now serve as a kind of revision heuristic, as an invitation to experiment with the text through such questions as "Why did I decide on this order? Did I have a reason? What if I had done such and such?" But to learn how to experiment and to determine what questions to ask, the student writer needs to watch more experienced writers at work. The student needs to see not only the finished products of these writers or even their drafts, but also the routes by which they traveled. The instructor, in other words, should share his or her own drafts and question logs so that student writers can trace and analyze the instructor's critical thinking.

References

Faigley, Lester, and Stephen Witte. "Analyzing Revision." *College Composition and Communication* 32, no. 4 (December 1981): 400–14.

Murray, Donald M. "Teaching the Other Self: The Writer's First Reader." In *Learning by Teaching: Selected Articles on Writing and Teaching*, 164–72. Montclair, N.J.: Boynton/Cook, 1982.

Sommers, Nancy. "Revision Strategies of Student Writers and Experienced Adult Writers." *College Composition and Communication* 31, no. 4 (December 1980): 378–88.

2 Speaking and Listening Activities

Teaching Critical Listening

Mary Bozik
University of Northern Iowa, Cedar Falls

One of the most frequent applications of critical thinking is critical listening. Studies show that college students spend 70 percent of their waking day communicating; 14 percent of that time is spent writing, 17 percent reading, 16 percent speaking, and 53 percent listening (Barker et al. 1980). A large part of our listening time requires evaluation. Decisions concerning what to buy, for whom to vote, and what to do with our time are just a few of the situations in which an oral message must be critically evaluated and an appropriate verbal or behavioral response determined.

High school and college students, who are frequent targets of persuasive techniques, are also inexperienced at making adult decisions. Cognitively they are moving from concrete to abstract thought and thus are increasingly able to see implications, understand hypothetical situations, and view issues as multifaceted. A unit on critical listening at this stage of development could be essential to developing cognitive complexity.

Effective critical listening requires students to begin by evaluating the speaker or source of the message. Three considerations determine the judgment made about a speaker: credibility, purpose, and bias. The following activities can be used to teach these three concepts in the high school or college classroom.

Determining Speaker Credibility

Speaker credibility is determined by five components: competence, character, intent, dynamism, and likeability (Baird 1981). After students define and discuss these concepts, give them a list of names such as the one below. You might want to include people currently in the news and local figures.

How do you view the following people as speakers? Mark each
name favorable (+), neutral (√), or unfavorable (−) in each of
the five components of credibility.

Competence Character Intent Dynamism Likeability

Ronald Reagan

Jimmy Connors

Ann Landers

Joan Collins

Robert Redford

Diana Ross

Billy Graham

Dan Rather

After the form is completed, ask students to indicate how they rated
these people on each of the five components. Explore why one person
is seen as likeable and another not. The lack of agreement on judging
competence will make it clear to students that the evaluation of a
speaker's competence is personal. When discussing competence, ask
students to list the topics on which each of the people listed would be
competent. Discuss the halo effect used in advertising which results in
football players selling panty hose and actors selling coffee.

The final idea requiring elaboration is the effect the rating of
competency would have on listening to a speaker's ideas. Students should
learn from this lesson that they should critically examine each source
of information and that this examination should play a role in their
acceptance or rejection of the speaker's message.

Determining the Speaker's Purpose

Offer students practice in determining the purpose, whether stated or
implied, of a message. Point out that speakers sometimes state the
purpose clearly in a thesis statement early in the message, or they may
use an inductive approach which states the purpose in the conclusion,
or they may never state the purpose.

The reason someone is speaking is an important factor in evaluating
a message. A football player who is paid $100,000 to make a commercial
is motivated by different forces than a friend who tells you a certain
brand of panty hose is the best. This, in turn, should influence the
evaluation of the message and your response to it.

Read students brief passages which exemplify the three strategies. Three sample paragraphs are reproduced below.

1. If any of you needed a kidney or other vital organ to live, would you be able to get one? Would you know where to begin searching for information which would lead to obtaining this needed organ?

   These are questions many of us have never even considered. Yet, each year, in America alone, many people die with kidney disease because donated kidneys are not available. Now wouldn't it be nice—no; fantastic—to have a major role in curbing some of this tragic and needless dying? You can do just that. I'd like to show you how today. (Phillip Doughtie, "The Gift of Life," in Adler and Rodman 1985, 369–71)

Here the purpose (to encourage listeners to donate kidneys) is made clear in the speaker's introductory remarks.

2. "I'm useless until I've had my morning cup of coffee!" Does that line sound familiar? Most people realize that drinking coffee gives them a lift—it alleviates drowsiness and acts as a general pick-me-up. These effects are the result of a drug found in coffee known as caffeine; and what most people don't realize when they drink that morning cup of coffee is that they are ingesting a drug.

   Yes, caffeine is a powerful stimulant, found not only in coffee, but also in tea, chocolate, soft drinks, and a number of over-the-counter drugs, including wake-up tablets, diet pills, and headache and cold remedies. It is one of the most widely consumed mind-affecting substances in the world, and the effects of consuming too much caffeine are given the name caffeinism. In the past, caffeine has been regarded as a minor drug that does no real damage. However, accumulating evidence indicates that this belief is a misconception and that caffeine can be injurious to our health.

   In the next few minutes, I'd like to take a closer look at the effects of caffeine, at its consumption in our society, and at some solutions to the caffeine problem. (Christine Murphy, "The Caffeine Concern," in Lucas 1983, 381–84)

In this speech, the purpose is not stated explicitly at the outset but is revealed in the speaker's conclusion: "I urge you to assess and monitor your caffeine intake. . . ."

3. I am happy to join with you today in what will go down in history as the greatest demonstration for freedom in the history of our nation.

Five score years ago, a great American, in whose symbolic shadow we stand today, signed the Emancipation Proclamation. This momentous decree came as a great beacon light of hope to millions of Negro slaves who had been seared in the flames of withering injustice. It came as a joyous daybreak to end the long night of their captivity.

But one hundred years later, the Negro still is not free. One hundred years later, the life of the Negro is still sadly crippled by the manacles of segregation and the chains of discrimination. One hundred years later, the Negro lives on a lonely island of poverty in the midst of a vast ocean of material prosperity. One hundred years later, the Negro is still languished in the corners of American society and finds himself an exile in his own land. And so we've come here today to dramatize a shameful condition. (Martin Luther King, Jr., "I Have a Dream," in Lucas 1983, 373–76)

King's purpose is not stated explicitly. He speaks of coming to Washington "to dramatize a shameful condition" but does not state the actual purpose of this speech. Most critics agree that the speech was designed to inspire the audience to continue to fight for equal rights.

After students have discussed brief passages like those above, have them read and discuss a longer message, such as a speech from *Vital Speeches of the Day* or from a college speech textbook, which will often label such components as the thesis, purpose sentence, main ideas, supporting materials, etc. A passage from a work of literature could also be examined from this perspective, using the dialogue to determine the speaker's purpose.

Determining Speaker Bias

A third consideration when listening critically to a speaker is identifying speaker bias. Typical sources of bias include personal experience, educational background, position or job, and self-interest. Ask students to cite instances where these factors influenced what they said. Then give students the following assignment to explore the concept of bias from the listener's perspective.

For each of the following claims, list a speaker who you feel would be biased and one who would be relatively unbiased.

Claim	Biased Speaker	Unbiased Speaker
The Academy Awards are meaningless.		
You should have a dental checkup every year.		
The well-dressed man of today wears an earring.		
Michael Jackson has had a greater effect on music than did the Beatles.		
You should smoke pot.		

Conclude the assignment by discussing with students how they should listen differently to a biased speaker than to an unbiased one. Point out that a biased speaker may still be honest and credible, but that the listener should listen carefully for supporting evidence for the speaker's ideas and should verify the message with his or her own experience. Encourage students to seek out various opinions on a topic, thus lessening the impact of a particular speaker's biases.

References

Adler, Ronald B., and George R. Rodman. *Understanding Human Communication.* New York: Holt, Rinehart and Winston, 1985.

Baird, John E. *Speaking for Results: Communication by Objectives.* New York: Harper and Row, 1981.

Barker, L., R. Edwards, C. Gaines, K. Gladney, and F. Holly. "An Investigation of Proportional Time Spent in Various Communication Activities by College Students." *Journal of Applied Communication Research* 8 (1980):101–109.

Lucas, Stephen. *The Art of Public Speaking.* New York: Random House, 1983.

Each One Teach One:
A Peer Teaching/Learning Unit

Margaret E. Rinkel
Mahomet-Seymour High School, Mahomet, Illinois

Few junior high or middle school students would miss an opportunity to talk about something they know firsthand. Few would admit to lack of knowledge about some topic. In fact, classroom discussion quickly points out that all students know how to carry out some process, craft, or skill worth talking about. Thus, an activity-oriented unit based on every student teaching another student his or her special skill capitalizes on this potential fluency in oral and written form. In addition, the unit's problem-solving focus depends largely upon the logical thinking skills of setting a goal, narrowing a topic, identifying and sequencing steps, selecting and organizing materials, and evaluating results.

To prepare for the unit, engage students in a brainstorming session, listing on the board various topics about which they feel knowledgeable and comfortable. Topics will range greatly, from guitar playing to constructing a vintage car model, from mnemonic devices to computer programming.

Make a copy of this list of topics, perhaps adding a few additional skills to the list. Distribute a copy to each student the following day and ask students to number in order of preference three skills they would like to teach and to rank, again in order of preference, three skills they might enjoy learning. Use these lists to pair "teachers" with "learners." Each student should be assigned two topics—one to teach and one to learn.

After the topics and the student pairs are determined, give each student a lesson-plan handout that includes spaces to be filled in with name, date, topic, objective, materials, steps in the process, and evaluation. Note that the teaching time for each topic will be one class period. Then direct students to think through their individual teaching plans following these guidelines:

Step one. Fill in your name, date, and topic and write your objective or goal as specifically as possible. For example, for the topic "How to

Play the Guitar," the goal might be "to play the scale and one simple song on the guitar." For the topic "Sign Language," the goal might be "to demonstrate the sign language symbol for each letter of the alphabet and to sign the words *you, friend,* and *love.*

Step two. List the materials that you will use in teaching the lesson: paper and pencil, camera, computer terminal, macramé cord. (Each student is to furnish specialty items not available in the classroom supplies. The cost of film for a camera project, for example, might be shared between "teacher" and "learner.")

Step three. Go through the process or craft that you plan to teach, listing and numbering each small step from start to finish. Since this is the most detailed and difficult part of the assignment, check your written steps with the instructor to avoid such directions as "Take the box of cake mix, place in pan, and bake at 350°."

Step four. Teach your lesson to the learner who has been paired with you. You will have the entire class period to teach the process or skill. On the following day, those who were teachers will shift roles with the learners, and the process is repeated.

Step five. Evaluate the learner's progress in learning your skill or process by having him or her demonstrate, translate, play, recall, or take a quiz.

Step six. Evaluate your teaching plan by writing one or more sentences in response to these questions:

How do you feel about the way the lesson turned out?

Did you reach the objective stated at the beginning of your plan?

How do you know that the learner actually learned the skill?

Would you change any part of your lesson plan if you were to teach this skill again? If so, how?

In a fun-filled way, students extend their knowledge and understanding of a subject through teaching and learning. As they teach, they are actively involved in explaining the process or craft, answering questions, correcting errors, reinforcing appropriate responses, and evaluating progress. For two weeks of intensive verbal and written skill building (minus groans), the total effect is decidedly positive.

Teaching Thinking through Questioning: A Collaborative Classroom Project

Mary H. Oestereicher
Brooklyn College, City University of New York

The extensive study of the nation's seventeen year olds conducted by the National Assessment of Educational Progress (1981, 2) suggests key problems in reasoning skills: ". . . responses to assessment items requiring explanations of criteria, analysis of [a] text or defense of a judgment or point of view were in general disappointing." These findings suggest that students generally lack many of the abilities which the College Entrance Examination Board (1983, 9–10) identifies as necessary reasoning skills for entering college freshmen:

> the ability to identify and formulate problems, as well as the ability to propose and evaluate ways to solve them
>
> the ability to recognize and use inductive and deductive reasoning, and to recognize fallacies in reasoning
>
> the ability to draw reasonable conclusions from information found in various sources, whether written, spoken, or displayed in tables and graphs, and to defend one's conclusions rationally
>
> the ability to distinguish between fact and opinion

An important area in the effort to develop student reasoning abilities, and one particularly suited to the English classroom, is questioning.[1] This chapter describes a classroom questioning project that involved college freshmen. It shows a method for developing students' critical thinking through their involvement in a collaborative process of creating, evaluating, and ordering questions and then pursuing the answers through interviews. The reasoning abilities especially targeted for development here were making judgments and providing evidence in defense of one's conclusions.

In this project, students were instructed to formulate and decide collectively upon a set of questions to be asked of upperclassmen regarding college life. Each student would subsequently select a junior or senior, ask him or her the questions, record the responses, and report back to the class. The focus of this chapter is on the class's formulation of the set of questions. The project, which took advantage of the dynamics of the whole class and the interests of college freshmen, was easily integrated into an English course (Oestereicher, in press). Students devised questions of importance to them and had great interest in the responses.

Procedure

Students determined their list of questions through collective deliberation. The instructor's role was to establish structures for the formation of the questions and to provide feedback during the deliberations. The process of determining the list of questions involved the following steps.

1. Posing the Problem

First the class briefly discussed some of the differences between how college life might seem to an entering student and to a junior or senior who has attended the college for two or three years. Then the instructor helped narrow students' thinking about college life by asking: "If you had a chance to ask an upperclassman about life at this college, what would you ask? Be sure to inquire about both academic and nonacademic concerns."

2. Generating the Questions

Each student was paired with another student. The partners were to develop a list of questions about college life that they would like answered. Potential questions were to be recorded as the partners discussed the topic, and by the end of the allotted time each pair of students was to have prepared a written list of questions that the pair wanted answered.

3. Writing the Questions

The next step in this cooperative venture was for one student from each pair to write their questions on the chalkboard.

4. Reading and Discussing the Questions

At this stage everyone would function as a critical reader of the questions on the board, with students taking turns reading questions aloud. Such review and reevaluation of writing, as Emig (1977) has noted, are important steps in developing critical thinking. The students eagerly turned their attention to such details as word choice or punctuation whenever anyone was unable to understand a question. In those cases, feedback from the class helped the writer rephrase the question to make it meaningful.

5. Revising the Questions

The next task for the group was to revise the set of questions on the board and to reduce their number. Clearly no one wanted to ask all those questions in their unrevised form. The students decided that some questions should be eliminated because they were redundant or because they made the scope of the project unmanageable, some should be improved for clarity, more questions should be added, and so forth. Students supported their suggestions for revision with well-reasoned arguments showing how the revisions would improve the set of questions. Only strong arguments won the support of the class and the instructor. Decisions regarding both form and content were made. For example, when two questions were redundant, the class had to decide which question should be eliminated by comparing and contrasting the two and then evaluating the merit of each. Sometimes students generated a synthesis of the two, improving upon both questions. Also, the tone of the questions ranged from slang to formal, making it necessary for students to determine the purpose and the audience. Thus, while some students originally had been planning their questions for a particular upperclassman, they realized it was now necessary to move to a higher level of abstraction and to arrive at an imagined respondent common to the class.

6. Ordering the Questions

The questions needed to be arranged in the best order, which meant the class had to decide upon some principles for ordering them. The instructor asked what kinds of questions were listed, inviting students to categorize the questions. The class saw that some questions were "superordinate," some "subordinate." The students determined that the questions could be grouped any of three ways: (1) according to topic, (2) according to those that called for facts and those that called for opinions (or, as a variation of the latter, those that called for advice), and (3) according to those that asked for highly personal information from the respondent and those that asked for only relatively impersonal information.

All three principles of categorizing were employed in determining the ultimate order. The final questionnaire moved from the impersonal to the personal, clustering questions on topics and following up opinion questions with questions requesting supporting evidence. Indeed, as students considered how to use opinion and fact questions in concert, they devised some new questions requesting evidence. (The students continued the process of generating questions during their individual interviews with juniors and seniors, creating follow-up questions in response to answers they found of interest, and reported these responses to the class as well.)

By the time the list of questions was finalized, everyone could see the qualitative difference between the set of questions each pair of students had started with and the final set. That difference bore witness to the power of creative and critical thinking that can inform and influence collective decision making. Students were able to carry out their interviews with confidence in the questionnaire, because it was created and validated in a critically thinking group of peers.

Strengths of the Class Project

The development of individual thinking skills through group interaction was the goal of this questioning project. Together, students learned to consider what information to seek, the best ways of phrasing questions to obtain information, and the best ways of ordering the questions. In a classroom of "planned cooperation" (Slavin 1983), the thoughtful use of language was deliberately fostered.

An important component of this collaborative (Bruffee 1984) project was that it provided the students with a concrete situation which was relevant to them. The project worked especially well with first-semester freshmen, whose eagerness and curiosity about college life kept their interest high. A similar activity would seem appropriate for newcomers at the junior high or high school level. This writing/reading/speaking project can readily serve as a focus for early discussions about the diverse roles of language in daily life and the practical advantages of mastering our language. A major strength of the project is that it leads in a natural way to genuine enthusiasm as the students work together on a project of mutual interest to all.

Note

1. See, for example, the general discussion of questioning in Graesser and Black (1985) or the review of research on questioning in Wong (1985).

References

Bruffee, K. A. "Collaborative Learning and the 'Conversation of Mankind.'" *College English* 46, no. 7 (November 1984): 635–52.

College Entrance Examination Board. *Academic Preparation for College.* New York: College Entrance Examination Board, 1983. ED 232 517.

Emig, Janet. "Writing as a Mode of Learning." *College Composition and Communication* 28, no. 2 (May 1977): 122–28.

Graesser, A. C., and J. B. Black. *The Psychology of Questions.* Hillsdale, N.J.: Lawrence Erlbaum, 1985.

National Assessment of Educational Progress. *Reading, Thinking, and Writing: Results from the 1979–80 National Assessment of Reading and Literature.* Denver: Education Commission of the States, 1981. ED 209 641.

Oestereicher, M. H. "Freshman English in a Larger Context: The Developmental Education Program Approach at Brooklyn College." In *New Methods in College Writing Programs: Theories in Practice,* edited by Paul Connolly and Teresa Vilardi. New York: Modern Language Association, in press.

Slavin, R. E. *Cooperative Learning.* New York: Longman, 1983.

Wong, B. Y. L. "Self-Questioning Instructional Research: A Review." *Review of Educational Research* 55 (Summer 1985): 227–68.

Note on ERIC Documents

Documents indexed in *Resources in Education (RIE)* are denoted by a 6-digit ED (Eric Document) number. The majority of ERIC documents are reproduced on microfiche and may be viewed at ERIC collections in libraries and other institutions or can be ordered from the ERIC Document Reproduction Service (EDRS) in either paper copy or microfiche. For ordering information and price schedules, write or call EDRS, 3900 Wheeler Avenue, Alexandria, VA 22304 (1-800-227-3742).

Modified Oxford Debate for Advanced Ninth Graders

Fran Caldwell
Newport High School, Newport, Oregon

No other activity in my ninth-grade advanced English class provides more practice in all of the communication skills—reading, writing, speaking, listening, and, especially, thinking—than does the unit which we call simply *Debate*. In spite of the fact that it taxes their expertise to the limits, or maybe *because* it does, these advanced students (two to three years above average in reading and writing on standardized tests) love this three-week period of mad scramble to outresearch, outwrite, and outspeak their opponents.

The Debate Format

Though the formal Oxford debate format is the model for this exercise, I have modified it considerably to accommodate the peculiarities of ninth graders. Students at this age level—in spite of how well they may be able to read, write, and speak—demand material in smaller portions. An entire class period of any single activity will result in disinterested squirms and wandering minds after the first thirty minutes. Therefore, by reducing the usual ten-minute speeches to five minutes, I have cut the actual time of the debate in half; one debate actively involving four students with the rest of the class as audience takes a maximum of thirty-five minutes. I have also tried to enliven preparation time by intermixing work in the library, work in the classroom, and teacher presentations.

I begin the unit by defining *debate* as "organized argument between knowledgeable people." Speaking from handouts, I go over the essential terms and procedures. A videotape of a debate given the previous year is useful in demonstrating how the event actually proceeds. If a tape is not available, directions and explanations must be extremely clear because most ninth graders have never seen a debate other than the presidential debates held at election time, very different from our version.

Essential terms for the debate are defined on a handout as follows:

Controversial issue: a subject that can be argued and supported from opposing points of view.

Resolution (sometimes called the proposition): a statement which defines the nature of the controversy, is stated in the affirmative, and provides a basis for argument for or against.

Affirmative: the persons who uphold the resolution, who argue for a change in what presently exists.

Negative: the persons who argue against the change proposed in the resolution, who uphold conditions as they presently exist.

Definition of terms: a clear explanation of the resolution, defining and limiting ideas; it is the affirmative team's responsibility, but the negative team must approve.

Evidence: the material offered as proof in an argument; it can be in the form of: (1) quotations from authorities, (2) examples of actual situations or case histories, or (3) facts and statistics.

Status quo: a Latin term meaning the existing state of affairs, the present or the current beliefs and actions.

Burden of proof: rests on the affirmative, who must prove that the status quo is unsatisfactory and that the affirmative way is better; because the affirmative has a more difficult task, this side is given the advantages of starting and ending the debate.

Stock issues: those issues which must be proved by the affirmative— (1) the need for the change, (2) the practicality of the change, and (3) the desirability of the change.

Presumption: the assumption that the negative is "right until proven wrong."

Constructive speeches: given in the first part of the debate; they present the major arguments with evidence.

Rebuttals: given in the second part of the debate; the process of rebuilding after attack or defending from attack.

A second handout presents the order and time restrictions for the class debate as follows:

Part One: Constructive Speeches

First Affirmative	2–5 minutes
First Negative	2–5 minutes
Second Negative	2–5 minutes
Second Affirmative	2–5 minutes

Recess
Part Two: Rebuttals
    Negative   5 minutes
    Affirmative   5 minutes

Debate Units

The next step is for each student to pair up with a partner, an aspect
particularly appealing to students in this age group. They have one
another for moral support when the time comes for presentation, and
they have the fun of preparing together, often in a secret and excited
fashion, to "demolish" their opponents. Two can work up the competitive
spirit easier than one. I let partnerships be entirely up to the students.
Usually they have no problem, but a few may need a gentle push to
locate a partner. If the class count cannot be equally divided by four,
trios can be formed.

As soon as partnerships are determined, I put together the debate
units of four students (two sets of partners), appearing to do so at
random but actually placing the stronger teams against each other.

Now students meet in their debate units to accomplish three tasks:
(1) selecting a current, interesting, and controversial issue, (2) writing
a clear resolution stated in the affirmative, and (3) determining affirmative and negative teams. This step is not easy, but after long and
serious discussion, usually noisy, the students make their decisions. A
list of possible resolutions can be supplied to speed up the process. If
duplication of issues occurs, the group reporting its resolution to the
teacher first has priority. Each finalized resolution can then be written
on the chalkboard, giving notice that the topic is taken.

Examples of popular resolutions include such topics as the following:

Resolved that mercy killing be legalized.

Resolved that capital punishment should be abolished.

Resolved that women as well as men should be drafted in time of
war.

Resolved that the 55 mile-per-hour speed limit be abolished.

Resolved that a freeze on nuclear weapons be instated.

Resolved that abortion for any reason be abolished.

Numerous other topics are possibilities, but students should be guided
to select issues on which sufficient information is easily accessible in the
school library.

Developing the Argument

Research is now the major task. Keeping well in mind the kinds of evidence necessary, especially in the affirmative's case, students begin the search. *The Readers' Guide to Periodical Literature* proves to be the most useful reference, although our school librarian keeps a well-stocked and up-to-date vertical file that is also valuable. Encyclopedias, almanacs, and books are always available, and some ambitious students have even conducted personal interviews with police officers, judges, and other authorities. Students take careful notes and make sure each item of information is documented; I have warned them that any undocumented material must be discounted if questioned by the opponent. I usually allow about five days for the research process. Ideally, the affirmatives and negatives should do their library research on different days, but it is not always feasible for a teacher to supervise two groups in two different places.

Partners should plan and rehearse their cases together. Approximately two days can be allowed in class for organizing and preparing the debate speeches. Usually students spend a considerable amount of time on their own as well.

Affirmatives must begin by defining terms and then proceed through each stock issue, giving their evidence as persuasively as possible. Negatives must defend the status quo and attack the contentions of the affirmatives. Partners can decide who will present which issues, but they should keep in mind that the strongest evidence is best presented last. I encourage students to put their speeches in outline form rather than writing out each word. The most effective speeches are not read, since good eye contact is necessary to be convincing.

During the recess, partners discuss ways to refute what the other side has said. Each side, of course, has made careful notes while the other side was speaking, and well before the debate the partners should anticipate their opponents' arguments as they plan their attack.

Rebuttals should follow a plan and may be given by one partner or shared by two. All points made in the constructive speech should be reiterated one by one, following each by what the opponent said to disprove it and then giving more evidence to reestablish it. A good rebuttal should end with a summary and a statement of the debaters' belief in the soundness of their argument.

Presentation

During the debates the debaters sit at their respective desks at the front of the room. They face their opponents, yet the desks are slanted

American Forensic Association Debate Ballot

Rank debaters in their order of excellence, starting with 1 for the best debater. *Rate* the debaters on the following scale:

A+ = 15	B− = 10	D = 5
A = 14	C+ = 9	D− = 4
A− = 13	C = 8	F+ = 3
B+ = 12	C− = 7	F = 2
B = 11	D+ = 6	F− = 1

	Rank	Rating
First Affirmative _____		
Second Affirmative _____		
First Negative _____		
Second Negative _____		

Resolved that _____

Comments:

First Affirmative	First Negative
Second Affirmative	Second Negative

Figure 1. Sample form for ranking and rating debaters.

enough so that the audience can see the debaters' faces as well. They are reminded to speak in loud, clear voices, with correct pronunciation and appropriate expression. Strict formality is upheld: the debaters and their positions are introduced to the audience; an official timekeeper watches the clock and warns debaters nonverbally when they reach the last minute of their time allotment; and only debaters are allowed to speak except during the recess.

A schedule is drawn up so students know on exactly which day they will debate. Depending on the length of class periods, one or two debates can take place each day. If time permits, it is interesting after each debate to allow questions or comments from the audience for the debaters to field.

Five judges should be selected from outside the class and allowed some time to familiarize themselves with the judging form. I usually ask upperclassmen to judge, but counselors, principals, vice-principals, custodians, other teachers, and even parents can often be recruited. Only one judge is needed for each debate. The judge uses the debate form in Figure 1, which was devised by the American Forensic Association. It allows space for each debater's name, a statement of the resolution, a ranking (first, second, third, and fourth) of each debater, a rating (points equated to letter grade) of each debater, and comments about each debater. At the conclusion of the debate and after the form is fully completed, the judge must also select either the affirmative or the negative team as the winner. This conclusion is written at the top of the form and circled; the judging form is then posted on the bulletin board.

Conclusion

Debate has proved to be one of the year's most successful activities, and the wide variety of skills it requires makes for good practice in communication and critical thinking. I often teach the persuasive essay at the conclusion of this unit because not only have the students already formulated a strong thesis statement and collected a set of supporting details, but they have learned the value of presenting material logically and clearly.

3 Activities to Accompany Literature Study

Three *R*'s for Critical Thinking about Literature: Reading, 'Riting, and Responding

John W. Swope
Prescarch, Inc., Aikcn, South Carolina

Edgar H. Thompson
Emory and Henry College, Emory, Virginia

Once upon a time teachers taught literature as a body of content to be mastered. The old paradigm was simple: teachers assigned literature; teachers and students read the assignment; then teachers told students what they had read. Although the old paradigm had some merit, it frequently made literature a threat to students, implying that they could not trust their own judgment about what they had read. The traditional lecture-discussion of *The Scarlet Letter,* for example, too easily became a collection of the *teacher's* random thoughts, more accurately titled "What *I* Think Hawthorne Really Meant When He Wrote."

Instead of the old paradigm, which allowed students to remain passive, we want to suggest an alternative approach that helps students to think actively about literature, that is, to engage in active reading of the text, to respond to and interact with it afterwards, and to explore its meaning through class discussion. Our adaptation of Stauffer's (1975, 44) predictive reading strategy helps launch students' reading. A reader-response journal, derived from Bleich (1975), allows students to record their reactions to the text in preparation for class discussion. And questioning strategies from Christenbury and Kelly (1983) provide a means to guide the class discussions. With these exercises as a foundation, students can engage in follow-up writing assignments about the literature. Once in place, this approach structures classroom activities, whether used with one selection or for all the literature covered in the course.

Predictive Reading

Originally developed in the elementary classroom, the predictive reading strategy is comparable to what children do when they read without any intervention. Teachers guide children as they read, helping them assimilate new information as they encounter it. In literature courses, intensive questioning of the students while they read a complete work is frequently impossible. An instructor can take a few minutes at the end of a class, however, to set up the reading of short works to be discussed for the next class. In a few minutes, the instructor can help the students begin to focus their reading by directing them to look at the title of a work and ponder the meaning of it. Then the students can read the first paragraph or stanza and question what seems to be happening and what might happen. On their own time, students can read the selection to determine whether their predictions were correct or not, altering these predictions as necessary. Consider the following prereading exercise for William Faulkner's "A Rose for Emily."

1. Read the title. What images or ideas does the author's title suggest? Who is Emily? Why does someone want to give her roses?

2. Read the first paragraph:

   > When Miss Emily Grierson died, our whole town went to her funeral: the men through a sort of respectful affection for a fallen monument, the women mostly out of curiosity to see the inside of her house, which no one save an old manservant—a combined gardener and cook—had seen in at least ten years. (211)

3. Were your original predictions accurate? In what ways were they not? What new predictions can you make based upon what you now know?

The students should continue this predictive process as they read, recording their responses in the text or in a separate reading journal.

Prediscussion Writing

After students read a work of literature, they need to connect the literature to their own experience. We believe that a reader-response journal allows students to make these connections. In the journal, students make three types of responses to each selection that they read: emotional, associative, and figurative (Bleich 1975). The emotional response clarifies the readers' immediate feelings about the literature, allowing readers to analyze and make sense of their subjective reactions. Although the associative responses may appear to be idiosyncratic and meaningless at first, they are important. They relate the experience of the reading to some part of the readers' subconscious experiences. We have found that students need to make at least five associations to ensure sufficient personal connections. The figurative response asks students to identify a feature—a word, phrase, theme, motif—and attempt to identify why that feature attracted their attention. The following is a sample journal response to "A Rose for Emily."

> *Emotional Response:* Sleeping with a corpse is demented. Small wonder the neighbors complained about a smell—it was Homer Baron rotting away in that boudoir. The old lady certainly did love to have an air of mystery about her, even before she killed the man who would have jilted her.

> *Associations:* (1) Seeing corpses of my father and other family friends in open caskets; (2) trying to polish the family silver for the first time in five years; (3) the town rebuilt the sidewalks on our block last summer and it took three weeks; (4) I remember the old Victorian styled houses in my grandfather's neighborhood in Lynchburg; (5) giving roses to my girlfriend when I was in college.

> *Feature:* The poison that Miss Emily gets at the pharmacy is labeled "for rats." Obviously, Miss Emily plans to use it to kill rats. In retrospect, she did. She used it to kill a figurative rather than literal rat—Homer Baron.

After making these responses, students are more aware of how the reading relates to their experiences and also better prepared to begin interpreting and evaluating the literature when they come to class. The teacher should also encourage students to note troublesome passages. We have found that students' questions about such passages are often better than the ones we might pose.

Questioning during Class Discussion

Contrary to what many teachers may think, questioning is both an art and a skill that requires preparation before each class. Several theorists have organized questions into hierarchies, but as Christenbury and Kelly (1983, 3–5) point out, using the term *hierarchy* implies one kind of questioning is superior to another. In fact, all kinds of questions are important in a discussion. Christenbury and Kelly believe that questions asked during any discussion should relate to three areas: the matter under discussion, the personal reality of the student, and the external reality of the world (12–13). In literature, *the matter* is *the text*, the *personal reality* is *the reader*, and the *external reality* is *the world/other literature* (15). Christenbury and Kelly suggest that in preparing questions for discussion, the teacher should think of the text, the reader, and the world/

other literature as intersecting circles. The instructor formulates *white questions* from any of the individual circles and *shaded questions* based upon the intersections of any two of the circles. The conjuncture of the three circles provides what Christenbury and Kelly call a *dense question* that includes the elements of all three circles, providing the focus for the class discussion. Both the white and shaded questions illuminate the issues embedded in the dense question. By the end of the discussion, students can give relatively sophisticated answers to the dense or central question. Consider the following questions about Faulkner's "A Rose for Emily."

White Questions

The Matter: What does Miss Emily say to the aldermen when they come to see her about her delinquent taxes?

Personal Reality: When do you feel that social class distinctions, such as those condemning Homer Baron as a Yankee, are discriminatory?

External Reality: Among the genteelly poor Southern aristocrats, what were the prevailing attitudes toward outsiders during the two generations following the Civil War?

Shaded Questions

The Matter/Personal Reality: Do you find, as Miss Emily did, that denial of a problem is a successful means of coping with it?

Personal Reality/External Reality: If you found yourself in love with someone who was socially unacceptable and who later spurned you, would you take revenge on him or her?

The Matter/External Reality: What were the social expectations of the post-Civil War South that influenced the people's reactions to Miss Emily's being courted by Homer Baron?

Dense Question

The Matter/Personal Reality/External Reality: Given the times in which she grew up, her age, and what was expected of her as a member of the town's upper class, would you convict Miss Emily for taking her revenge upon Homer Baron?

Although teachers should prepare all these questions before the class discussion, the dense question is the only one that needs to be presented to the students as an advance organizer. The dense question is not the end product of the discussion but the central focus of it. During the discussion, the students should explore all three elements: the matter, the personal reality, and the external reality (Christenbury and Kelly, 16).

In the teaching of literature, both the teacher and students have potentially meaningful responses to the written word as they connect the literature with their own experiences. The teacher's experience with literature is not necessarily better but more extensive. For teachers of literature, then, the task is not to pound the interpretation of a text into students' heads but to help students explore the literature and make meaningful connections between it and their lives. When teachers use the processes that we have described, the chances are greater that students will leave the literature classroom not only with both the desire and the confidence to continue reading but also with the skill to think critically about what they have read.

References

Bleich, David. *Readings and Feelings: An Introduction to Subjective Criticism.* Urbana, Ill.: National Council of Teachers of English, 1975.

Christenbury, Leila, and Patricia P. Kelly. *Questioning: A Path to Critical Thinking.* Urbana, Ill.: ERIC Clearinghouse on Reading and Communication Skills and National Council of Teachers of English, 1983.

Faulkner, William. "A Rose for Emily." In *Short Stories: A Study in Pleasure,* edited by Sean O'Faolain, 211–20. Boston: Little, Brown, 1961.

Stauffer, Russell G. *Directing the Reading-Thinking Process.* New York: Harper and Row, 1975.

Experiencing Contemporary Drama

George Klawitter
Viterbo College, La Crosse, Wisconsin

Teaching "theater of the absurd" plays can be a painful experience for teachers who encounter students looking for logic in literature. Accustomed to hunting for meaning in poems and short stories, young people can be exasperated by sequences in modern plays which seem to be unrelated to reality. After all, television, movies, and adolescent fiction reinforce the thinking patterns which produce their heroes and their villains. Students enjoy Big Bird as well as Matt Dillon because, fictive or fleshy, the characters reason the way students are taught real people reason. When, therefore, our students first come up against absurdist drama, they are likely to be dismayed, if not terrified. It is not easy for anyone, young or old, to watch the structures of language and society crumble into the laughter of dark humor.

It is important, however, that we teachers bring our college classes in contemporary literature face to face with Beckett and Ionesco and Pinter because the influence of these playwrights on modern theater has been significant. It is not enough to let students read a Beckett play, nor can we skirt the issue by a half-period lecture or a printed handout on the movement. Since theater of the absurd is eminently actable, I believe it is in the best interests of students to experience the absurd. With the discovery of simulation as a teaching tool in the classroom, new doors have been opened, helping literature become alive for students. When classes dramatize segments of novels, students are encouraged to "live," if only for fifteen minutes, such roles as salesclerks, mountain climbers, and hospital patients, in settings as diverse as *The Adventures of Huckleberry Finn* and *One Flew over the Cuckoo's Nest*.

What simulation has done for standard fiction, I believe, can also occur with absurdist drama. I am not referring here to the classroom enactment of cuttings from *Waiting for Godot* or *The Bald Soprano*. That is the method of the drama coach and is, moreover, an expected technique in the classroom presentation of any drama. Applied to an absurdist play, it does little to enliven the actual techniques of the absurdist playwrights who depend, to some degree, on shock or surprise for their effects. What shock is there for a classroom of students who, having read a cutting from *The Dumbwaiter*, witness on the next day the odd permutations of the menu requests enacted before their eyes?

In order to achieve the real feeling of spontaneity for absurdist drama, I employ a classroom exercise for which the students are totally unprepared. At the beginning of the period I write four names on the board with a short description of each character we will have in our bus station "experience":

> Helen Kolinski—an elderly woman traveling from La Crosse to Green Bay to visit her sister
>
> Valerie Cartwright—the second runner-up in the Miss La Crosse contest, going to Milwaukee for a job interview
>
> Jim Osborn—a high school dropout who is "moving on"
>
> Toby Messerschmidt—a seminarian heading to Appalachia to work for two weeks with the poor

I tell the students to write on a sheet of paper one speech of three or four lines for each character. After fifteen minutes I have them tear the paper to separate each speech, and I collect the speeches one at a time so we end up with a stack of twenty speeches for each of the four characters.

By this time in the exercise, students are intrigued with the "production," and it is not difficult to elicit volunteers for the four parts in our play. I conspicuously shuffle each stack of speeches before handing it to an actor while I tell the students about contemporary experiments with "chance" music (orchestra parts written on 3 × 5" cards and shuffled before each performance of a work). I suggest that one of the beauties of absurdist drama is that the unexpected, even when illogical, carries meaning to a world in which the nuclear arms buildup and political machinations often masquerade as logical consequences of civilization.

The four actors assume their characters on chairs at the front of the room. On this simple stage I point out the furniture in the bus station, the ticket window, the boarding dock, and the street entrance. Since the writers of the play have been encouraged to include stage directions along with their speeches, it may happen that a prop will be needed for which I am not prepared. But somehow the actors always have managed, and the needed props surface. Once even a bucket of

Kentucky Fried Chicken appeared as Toby's lunch. Students are inventive, and when physical props do not appear to be available, mime is also an imaginative exercise that neither Beckett nor Pinter, I suspect, would frown upon.

The play begins and the inanities follow one upon the other. Actors speak at cross purposes to themselves, and speeches come out of nowhere and head in no particular direction. But it is amazing how often characters will "make contact" on stage. Both situations are valid to an "absurd" experience. The lack of direct communication helps students appreciate the contemporary message that "we just do not listen enough to each other." The surprisingly appropriate dialogue clearly illustrates the role of coincidence in our lives. Both messages are standard fare of modern drama. A typical exchange follows:

> *Helen:* She was a good girl, always wore yellow ribbons in her hair. I couldn't. Mine was so grey so one day I cut it off.
>
> *Valerie:* (*to Helen*) I'm going to see my grandma someday. She's dying. Isn't that a shame? Old people keep doing that though, for the attention.
>
> *Toby:* (*turning to Helen and shaking her hand warmly*) I couldn't help but overhear your conversation. I just want to say that we could use more people like you in the world. God bless you.
>
> *Jim:* (*replying to Toby*) Yeah, I really like this area, but I'm trying to get down South before I get pneumonia.
>
> *Helen:* These places never have any soap in the restrooms. (*pause*) If my sister doesn't appreciate this trip, I'll never speak to her again. Imagine going all this way to help her pick out tropical fish for her cat's birthday.
>
> *Valerie:* Excuse me, ma'am; you don't mind if I look at these brochures? I'm so excited!
>
> *Toby:* Deus ex machina. Deus ex machina.
>
> *Jim:* Hey, you over there. Shut up. You're too loud.

Sometimes the play becomes violent. One afternoon our play had both a purse snatching and a murder. Fortunately, two of our actors that day were theater arts majors and were not afraid to scream, stab, and fall dead. It is my experience that students are apt to do more hamming than called for by the script, so action has never been a weak area in the productions. After the "play," we discuss the techniques that emerged and relate them to a sheet of fifteen characteristics of absurdist drama, a list given to the class for a previous discussion of a

Pinter play. I end our period with a suggestion that the play we had created was *sui generis;* it could never be repeated. The students had created something truly original.

Students generally react positively to this activity. They enjoy the break from standard analysis, from digging for form and meaning. They like a chance to flex their creative muscles. Once while students were busy writing speeches, a sophomore mumbled to her neighbor, "This is stupid." I seized the moment. "Not stupid, Theresa—absurd." The class got the point.

Collaborative Interpretation

Sam Dragga
Texas A&M University, College Station

I didn't want to lecture to the college students in my introductory literature class. I figured these students were tired of listening to their teachers lecturing on literature—tired of and intimidated by their teachers' "professional" (i.e., "correct") interpretations of this novel, that short story, this play, that poem. I figured students might only learn what I thought (and what the professional literary critics I synthesized in my lectures thought) about a given literary text. They might never determine what they themselves thought about the literature; worse, they might never even think about the literature. They would never be actively engaged by the assigned readings, just passively indoctrinated by me. They would leave my course with lots of notes about the things I had said—notes to which they would never again refer following the final examination. And they would be critically unprepared for their next interaction with a different literary text.

I considered class discussions; this technique, however, was usually disappointing. With thirty or forty students, class discussions always deteriorated to either a conversation between the teacher and several especially perceptive or loquacious students or a question-and-answer session with the teacher asking the questions and only the especially perceptive or courageous students risking the answers. I was tired of this, and I figured my students were also.

I was familiar with Peter Elbow's *Writing without Teachers* and Thom Hawkins's *Group Inquiry Techniques for Teaching Writing*. In my writing classes, I was using peer editing; students liked it and thought it was genuinely instructive. So did I. I decided this collaborative learning might be equally effective in my literature classes.

Establishing Small Groups

The technique I developed is fairly simple. Following a single class period during which I discuss the major characteristics of a given genre (e.g., for the short story I talk about plot, characterization, setting, point of view, theme, symbolism, and style) and thus establish basic terminology, the students begin their examination of the assigned readings.

I divide the class into four or five groups with seven or eight students in each group. I can effectively monitor this number of groups, and the size of the groups is small enough to permit even reticent students the opportunity to voice their ideas but still large enough to give students the security of genuine group membership. Students remain in these groups for the entire semester, collaborating on all in-class exercises; this also inspires group cohesion and effective cooperation among group members.

Directing the Group Discussion

At the beginning of class, I write two questions on the chalkboard. These are usually general questions that might be asked about any literary text so that students develop interpretive skills clearly applicable to subsequent texts. (My quizzes and examinations ask similar questions, thus testing the critical skills developed through the collaborative interpretation exercises.) For example, on Hemingway's "Hills Like White Elephants" I might ask, "Who is the narrator of the story?" and "What is the significance of the title?"

The students then gather in their groups to devise collective answers to both questions and to determine the textual justifications for their answers. I allow fifteen to twenty minutes for this collaborative interpretation. Each group appoints a speaker who will explain to the entire class his or her group's answers to the questions and the textual justifications for the answers. (The position of speaker rotates so that each member of the group serves as speaker several times during the semester.)

I design my questions to elicit several possible answers and to keep students continually referring to the literary text in search of answers and their justification, as shown in this excerpt from a group discussion:

> "I think the narrator in 'Hills Like White Elephants' is a customer at a nearby table—just somebody listening in on the couple's conversation. He doesn't give us anything more than just what he sees and hears—no background or explanation. So he can't be omniscient."
> "Why do you say *he*? Do you think it's a man?"
> "Maybe it's the waitress."

"No, I don't think so. She would have to move around too much
and would have other things to do. She couldn't just stand there
next to the table and listen in on this conversation."

"Besides, the bar's in the other room, and she'd have to go in
there to get the drinks for the customers."

"Oh, right."

"Yeah, so it's got to be somebody sitting at a table next to them.
He gives us long stretches of their conversation."

"Yeah, every little detail."

"So do you think it's a man?"

"I don't know."

"He's probably a traveler—why else would he be in that train
station?"

"Yeah, and do you remember when he refers to the man as an
American? Could that mean the narrator isn't?"

"Not necessarily. But he's probably alone. If he was with somebody, he'd probably be talking to them, not listening to somebody
else's conversation."

"Okay, then the narrator is a single traveler, sitting alone at a
table near the couple, possibly a man, possibly a non-American. Is
he reliable?"

"Oh, I think so. He doesn't know these people, so there's no
point in his giving us a biased version."

"Yeah, he doesn't tell us what we should think. He just records
their conversation and leaves it to the reader to judge."

"Right. He's a traveler and doesn't know anything more about
these people than what he tells us. It's not like he's leaving something
out on purpose or trying to cover up something."

As this discussion illustrates, students meeting in small groups risk
voicing their opinions. In order to arrive at the required "group answer"
to the questions asked, students willingly exchange ideas, disagree with
each other, build on each other's insights, and support their interpretations with logical arguments and textual evidence. The experienced
or perceptive students in a group model the process of interpreting a
text for the less experienced or perceptive students in that group.

My job is to monitor each group's progress in answering the questions
and, when necessary, to offer suggestions or give direction to a group's
discussion. I should mention that students never spend the entire time
in their groups seriously addressing the assigned questions or discussing the assigned literary text. Approximately 25 percent of their time
is spent socializing. Such small talk, however, is crucial to building the
mutual trust and understanding that facilitates the group's discussion
of the literature during the remaining 75 percent of the time. And
certainly it is no minor achievement to keep students in a literature
class attentive to the assigned readings 75 percent of the time.

Oral and Written Collaboration

As soon as all groups have composed answers to the questions, the speakers explain the answers to the full class. At the beginning of the semester, I ask the small groups to formulate their answers orally, with the speakers taking notes and reporting extemporaneously to the class. Within several weeks, however, I require that the answers be written as brief essays: the students compose collaboratively and dictate to the speakers, who write down and read the finished essays to the class. Thus students engage in collaborative writing as well as collaborative interpretation: the skilled writers in a group model the writing process for the less skilled writers in that group.

Dynamic class discussion follows the presentation of each group's answers, as students challenge differing interpretations, acknowledge a missed piece of evidence, build again on each other's insights, and develop a critical consensus. This process inspires students to discuss additional aspects of the literary text during the remainder of the class period.

Conclusion

This process of collaborative interpretation thus teaches students the major objectives of the typical introductory literature class: (1) to examine literary texts critically, (2) to develop interpretations of literary texts, (3) to justify interpretations with logic and textual evidence, (4) to evaluate differing interpretations, and (5) to compose oral and written explanations of literary interpretations. It is successful in doing so because it minimizes the teacher's domination of the classroom and maximizes the participation of students. As students learn to write by writing and read by reading, they also learn to think, analyze, and interpret by thinking, analyzing, and interpreting.

References

Elbow, Peter. *Writing without Teachers*. New York: Oxford University Press, 1973.

Hawkins, Thom. *Group Inquiry Techniques for Teaching Writing*. Urbana, Ill.: ERIC Clearinghouse on Reading and Communication Skills and National Council of Teachers of English, 1976.

Adapting the Courtroom Trial Format to Literature

Michael Segedy
Colegio Roosevelt, Lima, Peru

Adapting the courtroom trial format to literature is a unique approach for combining composition with other aspects of English instruction in high school. In the precomposition phase of writing, the courtroom procedure assures a high level of student enthusiasm while also requiring students to use and develop refined skills of recording, analysis, and synthesis. In fact, before composing their rough drafts of summations to the jury, students undertake in-depth character analyses, diligently engage in notetaking, work on artfully linking their ideas together through formal debating technique and protocol, and practice orally their speech and rhetorical skills. A week of precomposition activities during the courtroom proceedings culminates in a writing project in which each student composes a persuasive essay in the form of a summation to a hypothetical jury. For the majority of students, few writing assignments have ever been clearer in establishing the relationship between the speaker's voice, audience, and purpose—the prerequisites for any good piece of writing.

Novels Suitable for Courtroom Adaptation

Though obviously not all novels contain the kind of conflict necessary for constructing trial cases, there are numerous novels that do. Likely prospects are novels that focus on crimes against society, nature, or individuals, especially challenging novels where the motive for the crime is complex and remains hidden from the lazy gaze of the superficially involved and uncommitted reader.

1. I Am the Cheese

A novel that I have found particularly adaptable to the trial format is Robert Cormier's *I Am the Cheese*. Here students are confronted with the kind of abusive power a government agency can wield when its power resides in the hands of officials who are more concerned with protecting the agency's reputation than with caring about the welfare of a young boy. The trial examines both sides of the issue, raising the age-old philosophical question of whether the end justifies the means.

Students assume that Adam Farmer, the teenage protagonist, has escaped from the institution where he has been involuntarily confined for the last two years. He has sought legal aid in order to piece together the mystery surrounding his confinement at the hospital, his father's whereabouts, and the role a Mr. Grey and the institution have played in the death of his mother. The three or four students chosen to play lawyers representing Adam bring to trial the agency where he has been unlawfully detained. These student prosecution attorneys work together to construct their case, identifying the specific crimes committed by the agency against their client. Through diligent research and scrutiny of key facts and events described in the novel, the prosecution garners sufficient evidence to support its case. Since the tapes mentioned in the novel will be introduced as evidence during the proceedings, the team of defense attorneys has the responsibility of explaining to the court the motive behind the institution's confinement of Adam and convincing the court that the institution had no direct involvement in the disappearance of Adam's father and the death of his mother.

Some of the students who are neither defense nor prosecution lawyers are assigned character roles and are required to collect data about their characters from the novel. During the course of the trial, they will be called on to serve as witnesses. In addition, they must create for their characters special data not provided by the novel. They are admonished that none of their imaginative fabrications may contradict facts about their characters as portrayed in the novel.

No one is left out. Students not assigned roles as lawyers or characters from the novel become research aides and are paired with either a lawyer or a character as a sort of understudy. In the event of the absence of a lawyer or character, the appropriate partner is expected to fill the vacancy. All students are required to write the summations to the jury. These are based, in large part, on the evidence that was established through the lawyers' examinations and the testimonies of the witnesses. Thus all students are to take notes during and in preparation for the actual proceedings.

2. Frankenstein

Another novel that has all the requisites for an exciting trial is Mary Shelley's *Frankenstein*. This novel allows students to reflect on our criminal justice system, the aim of which is to guarantee justice but which often becomes mired in questions about moral responsibility while pursuing justice. It is difficult for students to decide whether the best candidate for the defendant is the monster or Victor Frankenstein, the monster's creator. Both characters provide rich opportunities for in-depth psychological insights into personality, and neither is free from blame for the numerous deaths that occur. In fact, whenever the monster is chosen as the defendant, it is often Victor who finds himself on trial, attempting to defend himself from accusations of scientific and moral irresponsibility.

In past classroom trials, students have favored the monster for the prime role of villain. The defense, on behalf of the monster, had the arduous task of proving that there was sufficient evidence that the accused was driven to commit acts of murder by psychological forces outside of his control. He was therefore not responsible for his actions because he was insane at the time of the commission of the murders. The defense would ask the court to acquit the accused and institution-alize him until his illness had been cured and he was fit to enter back into society. Conversely, in this typical case the prosecution would attempt to prove that the monster was completely and unequivocally in control of his mental faculties when he committed the diabolical mur-ders. He was not under duress and was thus free from external forces. He was not only aware of what he was doing at the time of the murders but even premeditated some of them. The prosecution would argue that if the monster were judged innocent by reason of insanity, he would be free someday to go on another murderous rampage whenever he felt rejection. Instead, the monster should pay for his crimes with his life.

Along with a host of characters from the novel (Robert Walton, Victor Frankenstein, a magistrate, Victor's college professor, the little girl saved by the monster, Agatha, Felix, Mr. Delacy, a bailiff, the monster himself), two new characters must be introduced into the courtroom drama: a psychologist for the prosecution and a psychologist for the defense. Both witnesses will offer expert testimony about the personality of the monster. They are required to spend time in the library looking through *Black's Law Dictionary*, where they can find legal definitions of what constitutes insanity. Then they must undertake some independent reading on mental disorders such as psychopathic person-ality disorders and paranoid schizophrenia. The psychologists play a major role in convincing the jury of the defendant's guilt or innocence.

3. Brave New World

Still another novel with which I have had great success in adapting the trial format to literature is Aldous Huxley's classic, *Brave New World*. Here, students must ponder whether stability and happiness are more important than freedom. In order to create a sense of verisimilitude in trial proceedings based on this novel, it was necessary to devise a situation that would give some credibility to the idea of a trial taking place in a totalitarian society. There would have to be a purpose for the trial that would not distort the purported benevolent aims of Brave New World. The following idea was adopted.

Every year dissidents of Brave New World are brought before a court-appointed judge (an Alpha +) who hears treason cases. The trial is closed to the public. Those present consist of witnesses for the defense and prosecution, neutral witnesses, lawyers, court clerks and officials, and a twelve-member jury consisting of former world controllers and regional directors. The purpose of the trial from the state's point of view is to determine the possible (yet highly improbable) legitimacy of the defendants' criticism and hostility toward Brave New World so that the leaders can discuss any need for change. The accused are Bernard Marx, Helmholtz Watson, and John Savage. (Obviously, John's suicide must be overlooked during the trial.)

Once the purpose for the trial is clear to the students and they are assigned roles, the prosecution and defense can begin constructing their cases. By working together in groups and participating in class discussion, students are able to construct arguable cases. The prosecution attempts to show that dignity and purpose are relative concepts belonging to a barbaric time in the past and that the survival of civilization is more important than such abstract principles as freedom and self-worth. Identity, Stability, and Community are the ultimate foundation for any society that hopes to survive. The aim, then, of any society is to reduce, or eliminate, human misery and suffering in the world. Brave New World has done exactly this. The three defendants on trial have tried to destabilize the society simply because they were more concerned with their personal freedom and individual welfare than the overall good of society.

Unlike in other trials, here the defendants must serve as their own defense. This eliminates uncontrollable bias on the part of any member of the Brave New World society chosen to defend them. The defendants will try to prove that Brave New World—by controlling individual destinies, diminishing the intensity of human emotions, promoting drug use for its citizens, destroying the notion of family, reducing the role of art to trivial and mindless entertainment, and assuming the role of God—has denied its citizens, for the sake of "Identity, Stability, and Community," any sense of purpose, dignity, or individual worth. They will argue that the defendants were only trying to make the leaders and citizens of Brave New World see the moral and spiritual harm this society is inflicting on its people.

The characters who play major roles in the trial can be grouped in three categories: witnesses for the prosecution, witnesses for the defense, and neutral witnesses. Lawyers are allowed to consult with their witnesses but not with neutral ones. This adds an element of spontaneity and unpredictability to the trial.

Summary

In addition to teaching students composition and rhetorical skills, a courtroom trial approach to literature demands that students explore both sides of such complex issues as morality and justice. In the process, they discover through literature how complicated life in the real world can be. They learn that legal and moral questions do not have simple answers. Alfred North Whitehead expressed it well when he once said, "There are no whole truths; all truths are half truths. It is trying to treat them as whole truths that plays the devil."

Collection, Connection, Projection: Using Written and Oral Presentation to Encourage Thinking Skills

Joseph F. Bonfiglio
Green Mountain Union High School, Chester, Vermont

Every fall I tell the high school juniors in my world literature class that my primary goal is to get them to think. Fellow teachers and parents have told me that I am attempting the impossible, but I have experienced success in reaching this goal by using writing and oral presentation as vehicles for practicing thinking skills.

We study world literature chronologically, and I preface each age with an overview of the philosophers who were influential during this period. I am selective and limit the presentations to a specific area. For example, since philosophy, in general, is the search for the ideal, I begin the course with Confucius and his utopian concept of "Li." When we study Greece and Rome, we discuss Aristotle, Plato, and Lucretius and their definitions of happiness. We also focus on Aristotle's definition of tragedy and tragic hero and Plato's myth of the cave and political system. When studying the neoclassical period, we focus on Descartes's and Pascal's discussions of reason versus emotion. These presentations are somewhat superficial but are highlighted by a film or a short reading selection.

The next step is to show how the literature and philosophy of an age are intertwined. During the Greek and Roman unit, the class reads three tragedies (*Medea, Oedipus Rex*, and *Antigone*). We discuss plot and theme, tie in Aristotle, and then go to work. My standard essay is "Who Is the Tragic Hero of _____ ?" I tell the students that they each must pick one character, and they must use the text and each aspect of Aristotle's definition of tragic hero to prove their choices. Because the students have the background of the discussion of Aristotle and their notes on his *Poetics*, most experience quick, painless success. Not only do they feel they can do this type of logical argument, but they feel they can do it well. I also like to plant a seed of doubt in their minds. When they write their first essays, which concern *Medea*, most of the students say Medea is the tragic hero. Using an overhead projector, I argue that Jason fits Aristotle's criteria more completely.

A parallel writing activity follows our discussion of Plato's idea for a political utopia. I ask the class to write whether they would like to live in this society and to imagine their role within it. Students share their papers with the class. Of course, the majority of the students who choose to accept Plato's political system picture themselves in the upper echelon of the society, which would make the system top-heavy and unviable. The discussion helps students recognize that they probably would not attain this high status if this system really worked. They also come to conclusions as to why Plato's two attempts at bringing his ideas to reality in Syracuse failed despite governmental assistance.

My favorite writing assignments are drawn from Chaucer and Boccaccio. After students have read the tale in which the Wife of Bath states that women desire dominance over men, I ask the class to write an essay on the topic "What Do People Really Desire Most?" The answers must be limited to one specific desire, supported by reasons and illustrated by incidents and examples. Some students say people desire money. Others opt for happiness or love. Still others cite security as the most desired object. After all the papers are read aloud, students are grouped according to their most desired object. Each group verbally "slugs it out" with the others, pointing out the superiority of its choice. By the end of the discussion, some students have changed sides, while others feel assured of their righteousness, but all have been involved in a situation requiring various levels and types of thinking.

When presenting Boccaccio's *Decameron*, I describe it as a group of one hundred stories examining human lust and folly. The stories are divided into ten thematic units, ten per unit, and each unit represents one day. I explain that Day 1 deals with the theme of religion and Day 2 concerns happy endings to calamitous situations. The subject of Day 3 is the attainment or recovery of a much desired thing. Day 4 concerns tragic love affairs, and Day 5 pertains to happy endings to unlucky love affairs. Clever retorts to insults is the subject of Day 6. Days 7 and 8 deal with deceptions practiced by wives upon their husbands and by men and women upon each other. Day 9 has no set theme (we call it "freestyle"), and Day 10 deals with the theme of generous behavior. The class then reads the story "The Three Rings" aloud. At the completion of the reading, I ask the students to tell me in writing the day on which this story was presented. I have already taken the precaution of removing all copies of *The Decameron* from the school library. I tell the students that they should not try to look up the day in *The Decameron* and that they will be evaluated on how they prove their choice rather than on the choice itself. (At least two or three students will tell me the next day that the books are missing from the library, although they were not trying to look up the answer when they discovered this interesting fact.) I eliminate Day 9 from consideration because it precludes the need for a choice. The students quickly recognize that days 4, 5, and 7 are not possibilities; but that still leaves six possible days.

These writing assignments have several common components. They require a choice. The students must understand that they can only select one alternative and must treat it with conviction. The assignments require the use of example and incident to illustrate the choice. They require logical development by means of fact and reason. They also require the verbal support of the individual or group. Most importantly, none of the assignments has one "right" answer.

The preparation of a written report is similar to the preparation of an oral presentation. Both require a complex thought process that is much more formal than the thought process required for daily speech or simple decision making. With this in mind, I carry my goal one step further in my senior advanced placement English class, which studies British literature chronologically. I explain to the students at the beginning of the year that I cannot possibly present all of the literature I would like to, so part of the responsibility falls to them. At the end of each unit, the class divides into groups of two or three students. Each group selects a piece of literature from a designated list. The list for the Renaissance might include *Dr. Faustus*, *The Duchess of Malfi*, *The Faerie Queene*, and *Epithalamion*. The unit on the birth of the novel might include *Robinson Crusoe*, *Gulliver's Travels*, and *Moll Flanders*. Each group must submit a written presentation to me and make an oral presentation to the class, complete with visual aids. The students' goal is to give the rest of the class some basic, working knowledge of the piece presented. They must choose the work of literature and the method of presentation; they must do the research; they must decide the thrust of the presentation; they must cope with the logistics of meeting together and working equally. The results have been diverse. My favorites have been a modernized, "Alice's Restaurant" version of *Robinson Crusoe*, with Crusoe living in an abandoned VW bus in the middle of Central Park, and a videotaped "People's Court" in which Orwell sues Huxley for plagiarism. I especially enjoy the sense of closure such a culminating activity provides. The students transfer their knowledge of the age we have just studied to a specific piece of literature, and they utilize the skills of judgment and inference, both sophisticated thought processes.

One of the two major projects of the year for these seniors is reading Thomas More's *Utopia* and creating a group utopia modeled after More's. The students must plan both physical characteristics of the environment and social and governmental behavior. I request that the students prepare an outlined overview of the entire society using such general headings as Physical Plant, Industry, Parenting, Economy, Recreation, and Government. Then I ask each group to focus in detail on one of the headings. Currently, I have five utopias displayed in my classroom: Terra Miranda, a tropical, recreation-oriented society with zero population growth and pure democracy; Sentry City, a socialistic oligarchy hidden in a mountain; TBC (Totally Benign Community), a domed island reliant on superior intellect and ESP; Project KS6-8, a space station complete with hydroponic gardens, intense education, and strict criminal justice; and Athalantis, a self-sufficient agricultural society. During their presentations, the groups are challenged by the other students and must defend the communities they have designed. The emphasis here is on creativity, yet the students are accountable for their logic and decisions.

During the course of the school year, most students progress from sketchy logical arguments to fully developed reasoning. They examine, employ, and question reason and logic and have fun doing so.

Write on the Reading!

Adele Fiderer
Scarsdale Public Schools, Scarsdale, New York

Why ask students to write to learn? Rather than simply reading a new subject matter in response to a teacher's questions and looking for predetermined right answers, students will learn more if they become actively involved with the written material by trying to interpret what they have just read.

I found a painless, even enjoyable, way to bring about this engagement between reader and writing by encouraging my students to talk back to the writer. They react to the text by writing on the page itself. For this purpose, I provide them with a duplicated page of the reading assignment. This means we aren't limited to reading textbooks; we use newspaper and magazine articles, excerpts from library books, even drawings.

In our social studies curriculum, my fourth graders studied Native American culture. I prepared for this unit by duplicating a description of the potlatch, a gift-giving custom of Northwest Indian tribes. I left wide margins around the printed text so that my students would have room to write their comments and questions on the paper. The excerpt included vocabulary and concepts new to the class; the youngsters would have to scrutinize the material closely to comprehend it.

First, using an overhead projector, I demonstrated how to do "think-writing" on a page of written material. On a transparency of the page, I wrote the word *why* next to the line that read "Everyone who received an invitation knew he had to accept or be disgraced," and I said aloud, "Why would people be disgraced if they didn't attend?" Then I circled the word *recipient* and drew a line to the margin, where I wrote, "Receiver? the person who got the gift?" I explained to my students that those were my guesses for the meaning of the word *recipient*. Near the end of the second paragraph I wrote, "Oh, this is one party I wouldn't want to attend."

BAD Potlach! *(handwritten title)*

Like the Sioux, the Northwest Indians held give-away feasts, known as "potlatches," but they were given in a much different spirit from those of the Sioux. A potlatch began when a man decided to make a public announcement that he had the right to some very important name, like Always-Giving-Away-Blankets-While-Talking, Too-Rich, From-Whom-Presents-Are-Expected, or Throwing-Away-Property. To assemble his guests, among whom he always numbered his greatest rivals and enemies, he sent messengers by canoe, sometimes hundreds of miles. *(handwritten: not clear)* *(handwritten: Wow!)*

Everyone who received an invitation knew he had to accept or be disgraced. Guests came with no spirit of celebration, for they had to eat everything that was put before them, no matter how uncomfortable it made them. They had to listen to long, insulting speeches from their host, who bragged insufferably about the greatness of his new name. *(handwritten: why be disgraced? why?)*

Worst of all was the time after the feasting when the host began to give gifts. To his worst enemy he presented the biggest pile of blankets or perhaps one of the copper plates worth several thousand blankets. The recipient knew that he must give a potlatch of his own and return a gift of much greater value than the one he had received. The host was really lending out blankets at interest, and custom required the guests to pay it no matter how exorbitant the cost. In the Kwakiutl tribe the rate of interest was one hundred per cent a year. If a man did not repay, he was utterly disgraced, and it sometimes happened that he sold himself into slavery in order to discharge the debt. *(handwritten: I hate slavery)*

Gifts were both a form of investment and a means of waging war. A rich leader in one village could get revenge on a leader in another by forcing him into bankruptcy. In addition, he might disgrace his enemy by showing how much property, in addition to the gifts, he could afford to destroy. He might throw a copper plate into the fire where it melted down and then dare any of his guests to do the same. He might tear up beautiful blankets, knock holes in the bottom of his best canoe, burn his house down, or even kill a slave or two. Guests who could not equal these feats of destruction went away in shame. *(handwritten: but Gifts Are Nice!!)* *(handwritten: That's Dumb)* *(handwritten: Thats Horible!)*

Figure 1. One fourth grader's "thinkwriting."

The ones that make,

Bankruptcy! *We had that to*

Why did the Indians pick that name?

Like the Sioux, the Northwest Indians held give-away feasts, known as potlatches, but they were given in a much different spirit from those of the Sioux. A potlatch began when a man decided to make a public announcement that he had the right to some very important name, like Always-Giving-Away-Blankets-While-Talking, Too-Rich, From-Whom-Presents-Are-Expected, or Throwing-Away-Property. To assemble his guests, among whom he always numbered his greatest rivals and enemies, he sent messengers by canoe, sometimes hundreds of miles.

why pick those kind of names?

Wierd names

The ones he didn't like?

Everyone who received an invitation knew he had to accept or be disgraced. Guests came with no spirit of celebration, for they had to eat everything that was put before them, no matter how uncomfortable it made them. They had to listen to long, insulting speeches from their host, who bragged insufferably about the greatness of his new name. Worst of all was the time after the feasting when the host began to give gifts. To his worst enemy he presented the biggest pile of blankets, or perhaps one of the copper plates worth several thousand blankets. The recipient knew that he must give a potlatch of his own and return a gift of much greater value than the one he had received. The host was really lending out blankets at interest, and custom required the guests to pay it no matter how exorbitant the cost. In the Kwakiutl tribe the rate of interest was one hundred per cent a year. If a man did not repay, he was utterly disgraced, and it sometimes happened that he sold himself into slavery in order to discharge the debt.

Ugh!

Why?

besides copper what kind of plate

Poor man! Very poor!

high cost?

Does it stand for anything?

Gifts were both a form of investment and a means of waging war. A rich leader in one village could get revenge on a leader in another by forcing him into bankruptcy. In addition, he might disgrace his enemy by showing how much property, in addition to the gifts, he could afford to destroy. He might throw a copper plate into the fire where it melted down and then dare any of his guests to do the same. He might tear up beautiful blankets, knock holes in the bottom of his best canoe, burn his house down, or even kill a slave or two. Guests who could not equal these feats of destruction went away in shame.

Waging?

I wouldn't ever do that!

Why would they be sad? shee h!

Figure 2. Another fourth grader's "thinkwriting."

As I distributed copies of the excerpt about the potlatch, I explained to my students that they were to write whatever came into their minds as they were reading. In a written dialogue they were to tell the author of the article what they thought about something they had just read and to indicate if they did not understand something the author wrote. If they came across unfamiliar words, they were to guess at the meanings, just as I had done. Since the excerpt had no title, they were to write a title in the top margin. I assured the students that there were no wrong answers in "thinkwriting," and that spelling, punctuation, and grammar did not matter here.

As the students read silently, they wrote. Many of their responses were questions about words and phrases—"What does that mean?"— accompanied occasionally by guesses. Other responses were comments about how the host of the potlatch, with much insult and boasting, would give away his possessions, which forced the guests to reciprocate with a gift of greater value, often causing bankruptcy:

> I would hate that.
>
> Why did they pick those kinds of names?
>
> Why couldn't they refuse to come?
>
> That's dumb.
>
> There goes his canoe.
>
> Why would he do that to his property?
>
> I don't understand that.
>
> I hate slavery.
>
> That would make him the best.

These brief written comments were visible and concrete evidence that each child had really tried to learn something about the potlatch. No two pages of "thinkwriting" responses were alike; each student had attempted to make personal connections between his or her own experiences and what the writer was saying about this custom, which seemed strange to the students. Two examples of "thinkwriting" appear in Figures 1 and 2.[1]

By circling phrases and sentences or by highlighting them with light-colored felt-tip markers, my students indicated to themselves and to me which parts of the excerpt had interested or intrigued them. The following day we discussed in small group conferences the words or phrases to which students had reacted by "thinkwriting." Their talk reflected true understanding of the reading. Students concluded the assignment by summarizing what they had learned and what their reactions were by writing once again, this time in their social studies journals.

"Thinkwriting" or writing on the reading has become a successful strategy in my class for introducing students to new subjects and for helping them learn through interpretation and commentary.

Note

1. The text I distributed came from Sydney E. Fletcher's *American Indians* (Grosset and Dunlap, 1954), 106–108.

The Spheres of Experience:
A Schema Theory for Writers

Jeanne Gunner
University of California, Los Angeles

Researchers in language skills tell us that students can read most effectively when they have some intellectual context, or schema, for their work. When students confront new information or think about a topic in what is to them an intellectual vacuum, new information and ideas often pass through their brains, finding no ready place to alight and be assimilated. We all know the feeling of confronting some new concept that seems totally foreign to our experience. Spend a few minutes talking to a chemist, an electrician, or a banker; if you are unfamiliar with physical theory, electronics, or high finance, you can quickly get an overwhelming amount of information that you may find vaguely apprehendable at the moment but whose sense seems to evanesce with the conversation's end. When we ask questions because they have personal relevance, however, and when the answers relate to some sphere of our experience, then the information "clicks." We can ask a pharmacist about how a new prescription should be taken and can understand why one compound must or must not be mixed with another; we quickly learn that electromagnetic or heat forces endanger our word-processing disks; the real estate market becomes vividly alive when it is our own home being bought or sold.

Even where we lack a sense of personal immediacy, when we don't perceive the new information to be directly relevant to us, we can still imagine a time when it might be, or we can empathize with its possible importance for another person, or we can enjoy the challenge of making the new familiar. By the time we reach college age, most of us have had enough experience in life to create a theoretical context for almost any new idea. These are attitudes that we can become aware of and can learn to use, making them techniques for receiving and storing new information. In turn, we can use that assimilated information as stimulation and background for new ideas as we write. Thus the college student who creates a hospitable atmosphere for the new information he or she wishes to gain from reading can also benefit by using a similar approach to writing assignments. Instead of trying to work within the confines of what may seem an alien topic, students can train themselves to begin generating ideas for writing out of what they already know— not only about the particular topic itself but about the world, how people perceive the world, and the kinds of experiences they commonly face in it. This technique, which I call a schema theory for writers, involves training students to think about their essay topics systematically as well as creatively, with the goal of making an assigned topic comprehensible, relevant, and unthreatening. I think the technique can be taught and encouraged in almost any class in almost all academic fields. Because I teach writing, I'll discuss how I teach my composition students to draw on their own spheres of experience to make writing and reading assignments easier to confront and complete.

Overcoming Students' Initial Resistance

In my developmental English classes, I believe in using truly academic, intellectually demanding material. The students read Plato, Voltaire, Freud, Pope, Machiavelli, Sartre; they write on myth, neoclassicism, genetic engineering, Marxism, terrorism; they analyze, define, compare, contrast, synthesize. Clearly, most of them have little familiarity with these names and concepts. Most of them assume they will never need to, want to, or possibly be able to use such information. So with each new reading and essay assignment, the first battle is with their own sense of predetermined dislike and defeat.

"I don't know history!" "I hate literature!" "I was never good at science!" Take a moment to look closely at the structure of these student comments. They reveal a sense of polarity on the students' part: in their own eyes, students are egos separated from a given academic field by their feelings of suspicion, hatred, and fear. This egoistic basis is a good place to start teaching the writing schema technique. When I hand out an assignment that elicits this kind of suspicious/hostile/ fearful response, I put the responses on the chalkboard (which depersonalizes them to a useful extent, so no student feels put on the spot). I ask the students to describe the feelings behind these comments. What usually materializes from our discussion is the recognition that there's a kind of intellectual bias at work. Like other forms of prejudice, intellectual bias is most often generated by unexamined feelings, not rational thought. I ask the students for possible ways of reducing bias. I usually focus on racial bias, since it's a topic most students are familiar with in various ways. People, students suggest, can be open to learning about others and can empathize with their situations, focusing on shared concerns instead of irrational fears. We then draw the parallel between bias in general and intellectual bias. The challenge is made without confrontation; students cannot afford to be intellectual bigots and must develop a way to take in what they may previously have rejected, been bored by, or found totally alien and mystifying.

Identifying Spheres of Experience

The next task is getting the students to apply this liberal attitude to their specific writing assignment. To begin the process, I ask students to name their spheres of experience. To reduce their initial perplexity, I may list a few ways in which we commonly experience the world, or I may ask them to list the ways in which they can react to a given situation. For example, I might ask them to examine their classroom roles. They are students first of all; what sphere of experience does that involve? "Education" is the usual response. So then we put *educational* on the board as a way of describing one kind, or sphere, of experience. The students are usually friendly with each other; *social,* then, names another sphere of experience. At this point, students start making numerous suggestions, such as this partial list of spheres that one class generated:

educational	racial
social	physical
romantic	historical
aesthetic	nutritional
financial	family
egoistic	intellectual
cosmetic	sexual
fantasy	professional
athletic	gender-conscious
religious	paternal/maternal
emotional	style/fashion-conscious
creative	neurotic
political	objective/rational

With each class comes a new list, a phenomenon that in itself illustrates the seemingly endless creativity of human perceptions and, in turn, of basic writers as well. The terms on the above list have been refined, a valuable exercise in itself, as students work to make their terms precise and thus develop their skills in abstract thinking. The exercise helps them move from informal speech to formal, written academic discourse. They transform a comment like "Well, you know, like when you're happy—not from doing anything but from think-ing . . . about things, not now, in the future" into the term *fantasy* or change "Well, you go to work" into the term *professional.*

Applying Spheres of Experience to Reading and Writing

One very practical value of the spheres-of-experience approach is that students have the raw material for the technique immediately at hand. An instructor can continually encourage this approach as a habitual way of thinking so that it's available to students as a conscious tool when they read and write. The technique also provides one solution to writer's block by helping to free a student's creative and analytic thought from restrictive patterns. More generally, it helps students find ways of exploring topics instead of simply supplying pat answers. In one par-ticular assignment, I asked my students to read a selection from Homer's *Odyssey* and then write a short essay analyzing Odysseus's motives for taunting the Cyclops, whom he had already blinded and tricked. By looking at the isolated incident itself, the students came up with routine responses like "he was stupid" or "to get the Cyclops mad." When we went through the list of common spheres of experience, however, the students were able to generate new, more interesting, and more sophis-ticated possibilities: from *family* grew the idea that Odysseus was trying to make his "family," his people, proud of him, look up to him, and accept his leadership by proving his fearlessness. He was celebrating his *creativity* in having played such a clever and effective trick. He was showing that the gods must think highly of him since he got away with conquering the Cyclops, who descended from gods (a point generated from the term *religious*). The students were able to envision Odysseus as a thinking, feeling, aware individual by transferring traits from themselves to him in order to get at his possible psychology. In this instance, the technique helped the students move from simple reaction/response through higher levels of thought to a written account analyzing Odysseus's behavior.

The benefits of the spheres-of-experience approach extend to read-ing assignments. Because students in my class are assigned readings that to them seem very difficult, it is especially important for them to have some way of demystifying the material. First I ask them to consolidate related information they already have on the assigned subject. When they were asked to read a selection from Castiglione's *Book of the Courtier,* for example, they first had to fill out a "reading sheet" consisting of such entries as "List other Renaissance works you've read so far in the course"; "Describe the Renaissance attitude toward religion"; "Describe the political atmosphere of a great monarch's court." All the directives related to readings they had previously done. By reading Castiglione in such a context, the students were better able to grasp his notion of "sprezzatura" and make inferences about the value of elegant speech and personal style in that particular culture. The students who ran into difficulty understanding the work objectively were able to apply the spheres-of-experience approach. They asked questions modeled after "How does a courtier feel about family?" substituting the categories we had listed on the board (e.g., *religion, love, art, ego*) for *family*. When a category seemed not to apply to the topic, they had to ask why not: was some other experience considered more valuable? A courtier clearly cared more for intellect, athletics, and style than for family and profession, for instance. In this way, no part of the process is a waste of time and effort, for the students get some specific result from each question they ask, which reduces the sense of frustration or defeat they may encounter as they read difficult material. Their work is also a prewriting exercise, for I follow it with a writing assignment that draws on the ideas they have already generated. The process makes reading and writing preparation truly feed one another, and both are supported by the students' original thoughts. Given a writing assignment that asks them to analyze the value of style first for the Renaissance courtier and then more generally for people today, the students—who have already read with a context, synthesized background information, and explored the topic from many different perspectives by considering their own spheres of experience—are ready to write intelligent essays.

Teaching thinking effectively seems to me to depend not only on finding the right techniques but on making those techniques habits of mind. Students should leave the classroom with more than notes and assignments: they need the intellectual training that allows them to transform information into knowledge and exercises into patterns of thought. The specific classroom practice I have described here provides this intellectual training, thus reinforcing one basic goal of higher education.

Thinking through Dilemmas

Ruth Vinz
Boise High School, Boise, Idaho

What a splendid idea Sartre had in *Nausea*. Remember the character Roquentin? His mind seems to split in half, which gives him the ability to run through the streets of Bouville feeling the cobblestones under his feet while he writes down the experience as it occurs. Sartre captivates us with this technique. We are drawn to this evocative sense of simultaneity, of experiencing and recording an experience. I'm left with a dilemma when I think about the incongruity. How can the mind adjust to these very separate dimensions working as one? Yet that is exactly what occurs. The notion certainly stimulates my thinking.

I want to understand how Sartre led me to believe that his character could act, react, interpret, and record experience simultaneously. I believe we have this power—sometimes. I started to think about ways to tap such potential in classroom activities.

I redesigned a unit in my literature and composition class for high school seniors after I thought about Roquentin and his multidimensional antics. The old unit centered on a study of Henry James's *Turn of the Screw*. We probed the mystery and then focused on critical interpretation of this short novel. Yes, we had some personalized interaction with the text, as Louise Rosenblatt would suggest. The culminating assignment was an interpretive essay.

In the new unit, activities build an awareness of how we think—the acrobatics and fluidity, the leaps of imagination, the grueling task of evaluation, the experiencing and recording and interpreting. Gymnastics of the mind, I'd venture to say.

Initial Writing and the Cataloging of Dilemmas

After we read *The Turn of the Screw* (many other novels or short stories would work equally well), exploration begins with three impromptu writing topics: "Are the ghosts real?" "Is the governess sane or insane?"

"Are the children guilty or innocent?" Writing serves as a tool for discovery at this point. Each question encourages students to think through the complexity of dilemmas introduced in the story. After fifteen or twenty minutes of writing time, students have a better grasp of the deliberate ambiguity and mystery, the uncertainties that carry no easy resolutions.

Stretch student imagination and thinking by following the impromptu writing topics with an oral cataloging of dilemmas in *The Turn of the Screw*. Students often begin with the governess, looking at her confrontations with the children, the ghosts, or herself. Then students move to less obvious confrontations: the uncle's lack of concern, the naïveté of Mrs. Grose, the letter from Miles's school. I record dilemmas on the board as students present them. Tapping the powers of the right brain, I end the cataloging with a visual demonstration as I prod for a kernel dilemma (e.g., knowledge versus innocence, good versus evil, imagination versus fact). Once we have established a core dilemma, I diagram, using concentric circles and connecting lines, the spiderweb of interrelated dilemmas present in James's story. With little prompting, students take the lead in this visual pursuit, seeking the interrelatedness of conflicting forces.

Students challenge themselves to add circles by constantly moving into subtle realms, building circles based on setting, on character action or lack of action, on the appearance of outside forces, on silence, and on extenuating circumstances. They speculate freely when pressed to add another layer. Structural dilemmas, such as the half-frame where a love-struck Douglas begins a story but disappears, never resurfacing, or the use of a manuscript rather than a narrator, provide students with new levels of understanding. Hidden dilemmas, the power of one dilemma to enhance another, and the root or related roots of key dilemmas all add new connections. Students build a visual diagram, a record of their journey through James's story, showing relationships with lines, stars, and arrows. I find that this visual record of thinking brings power and sureness to the students' imaginative quest.

Resolving a Dilemma through Oral Composition

Next I ask students to consider possible resolutions not given in the story. There is one wrinkle in the speculation—solutions cannot detract from the meaning or mystery of the story. "That is a tough proposition," students tell me. As students consider this next "turn" in our study of James's novel, I remind them that James tells us "the story won't tell"

(3). Exactly. Our new dilemma, one we will work with for the next several days, has been introduced.

I ask students to write an imaginative and speculative addition to the work that will solve one of the story's dilemmas before it happens, during a pivotal incident, or after the fact. As students create this new piece, they tap their own understanding of James's style, pace, and point of view. They engage in imaginative thinking when they consider possible additions, rearrangements, and deletions dependent on existing actions, characters, and events. Students fit their creative piece into the story line, matching the style so that a reader might not suspect a breaking point in the original. Some suggested topics include creating a dream sequence for one or more characters, writing a diary entry or a letter that reveals information, having a character make a discovery during the story, writing an end frame, and giving new action or speech to a character (e.g., a silent character might be given a voice). I know of no better way to have students exercise their imaginations while studying literature. In theory and practice, students discover new ways of thinking about James's novel.

I throw a final "turn" into this unit. Remembering the divided mind of Roquentin, I ask students to write their additions to *The Turn of the Screw* in an atypical way. Students are to do their initial drafting and related brain work *orally*. Most of us carry on internal verbalizations as we write, but the audience for these dialogues is ourselves. In this activity, the writer will have an external audience for this verbal composing.

The students form pairs. One partner is the writer for the next two days; the other is the eavesdropper and interpreter of the writing process. The writers are given a general way of solving a dilemma present in the story. For example, students might solve a dilemma by creating a new character whose arrival interferes with or changes an outcome, or students might change an action or reaction of any one character. I have several options in mind and use different alternatives for each member of the pair. Eavesdroppers in the first round tend to jump ahead and start working on the assignment if they know the topics will be the same for them, and thus they lose the benefit of spontaneous oral composing. Once writers have a clear idea of the options, I give the following instructions:

> Compose out loud. Say everything that comes into your mind. Get the workings of your mind floating in the air in front of you. Verbalize all of your thoughts. Write down what you normally would write once you have orally sifted the chaff from the grain.

This is a good time to talk with students about the critical part of the writing mind. Remind students how much time they spend mentally editing and critiquing before they put words on paper. Remind them of the opposite experience where "fast writes" or "brain writes" lead them into the creative part of their writing minds.

The listeners need instructions also. This group eavesdrops on the writers' oral thinking. While the writers say everything that comes to mind and then write down what they want in their first drafts, the listeners make notes. They observe the writers' thoughts, watch the writers' habits while composing, and interpret the type of thinking they observe. Listeners might consider how much time writers follow creative bursts, how much time writers spend judging and critiquing their thoughts. How much time at speculation? At evaluation? In a real sense, eavesdroppers provide a link between thought and the written product. Listeners should not interfere or interject comments. They serve as recorders of the composing process.

This exercise magnifies the working of the writer's mind, exploring and interpreting the unconscious processes of composing. It will help the student pairs develop sensitivity to the thinking that takes place during writing. One student recorded his partner Stacy's oral thoughts in this way:

> I'm intrigued by the uncle's silence in the novel and wonder if I can bring him into the story without ruining the atmosphere where the governess must function alone. I want to give her strength enough to control the situation . . . I must find a place where his intrusion would seem natural . . . Where are the places that might work? The uncle could bring Miles home from school; he could escort the governess to Bly and see Quint himself . . . no, all are too obvious. One of the children could write for help . . . might be the best of all . . . Uncle resolves not to go or aid . . . one place to start this strand would be at the end of Chapter XV. Start the hint where James writes ". . . he marched off alone into church." I'll add "and he later proved full wit at trying to get his uncle's attention, but of that I will arrive all too soon."

Stacy has begun with a thread of imaginative writing that will blend through several chapters. Her observer goes on to interpret her brain writing:

> Stacy is a cautious creator. She is careful in preparing; she scans sections of the book, pauses, looks at circumstances from many angles. When a thought strikes her, she talks it out. She says it aloud to try it on for size. Once she has verbalized ideas, she writes at a hurried pace. Then when the spurt of writing is finished, she slacks off on her pace, studies the passage and begins her search again.

Stacy reflects on her own experience:

> In the past two days, I learned something about myself as a writer.
> I see more of the process I go through. I feel as if I have been
> honest with myself. I know that I am stubborn in writing, that I
> need to be more flexible, to allow myself to move on when I'm
> stumped on a word or idea. It helps to bring my methods in the
> open where I can try to take advantage of my best patterns of
> thought. I started thinking about the critical/creative parts of my
> mind. I'll try new strategies each time I write.

The exercise is designed to make the unconscious conscious and the
internal external. After two days, the listeners discuss their reactions to
the writers' mental flurries. The pairs switch roles for the next two
days, receive new topics, and repeat the process. The actual writing of
the imaginative section of the novel is ongoing, as students rework and
refine their final compositions.

Such oral activity reproduces mental language and explores writers'
thinking minds. I believe this assignment alters students' sensitivity to
their thought processes. In a sense, these young writers experience
conversations with themselves. They have a record of the workings of
their imaginative and critical minds, the many chance associations, the
give-and-take as ideas develop. The sequence of logical thinking and
mental leaps provides students with the footprints of thought that help
carry these writers through the streets of their own Bouville. Through
the assignment, they develop better understanding of themselves as
writers and the writing process. My goal is to create increasingly fluent
improvisers, fleet of foot and mind like Roquentin.

Reference

James, Henry. *The Turn of the Screw.* New York: W. W. Norton, 1966.

4 Additional Creative and Critical Thinking Activities

Right On, Right Answers

Lee Mountain
University of Houston, Texas

Sharon Crawley
University of Texas, El Paso

Debbie is a joy to have in class—except during open-ended discussions. Just when the discussion is going strong, Debbie has a way of frowning, raising her hand, and saying, "You asked a question at the start of this discussion. So far, I've heard three different answers. Which one is right?"

Then, invariably, Debbie is joined by the other children in the class who want to be told the *one right answer*. Of course, there is not always just one right answer, but just try to convince Debbie of that.

Maybe, before Debbie's birth, her mother was frightened by a jigsaw puzzle. Maybe that would account for Debbie's conviction that there is always only one correct way to put the pieces together. Or maybe workbook exercises have given Debbie years of satisfying reinforcement for her one-way thinking. After all, for a true-false statement or a multiple-choice question, there is only one right answer.

But for open-ended discussions in such areas as language arts and social studies, Debbie needs to be able to switch gears. In these areas her one-way thinking is sometimes painfully inadequate. Literature preaches that the right answer for one person may not be the right answer for another. Open-ended questions are supposed to bring forth numerous "right answers," showing the diversity of thought within the group. The area of values clarification calls for each child to generate his or her own alternatives, so each child has to come up with more than one way to "put the pieces together."

Children need to be able to switch back and forth comfortably from one-way thinking, where they focus on the one right answer, to open-ended thinking, where they consider numerous possibilities, options, and alternatives. Since much of their schoolwork promotes one-way

115

thinking, many pupils share Debbie's discomfort at more than one right answer, so they need help in traveling on a gradual path toward open-ended thinking.

The following instructional sequence describes the first three steps on such a path. After these three steps, which move from the concrete to the abstract, pupils are often able to keep going on their own.

Step 1: More-Than-One-Way Puzzles

You can start with something tangibly concrete—cardboard puzzles. This is almost like starting in the enemy's camp since cardboard jigsaw puzzles usually promote one-way thinking rather than open-ended thinking. A few puzzles, however, can be put together in more than one way, as demonstrated by Joseph Leeming (1946, 111–17). Even primary grade children can take a step toward open-ended thinking as they learn to put each of the following puzzles together in more than one way.

Cross and Square Puzzle

The two shapes in Figure 1—the cross and the square—are made from the same four pieces, which have been put together in two different ways. Both ways are "right." To construct this puzzle, draw on graph paper a cross in which all lines are equal in length. Draw line AE connecting two corners of the cross. Draw line CG connecting the midpoints of lines BD and FH as shown and intersecting line AE at point A.

Pentagon and Square Puzzle

The puzzle from Leeming's book shown in Figure 2 also demonstrates that there can be more than one way to assemble four puzzle pieces. To construct this puzzle, draw on graph paper a pentagon in which lines AB, BC, and AF are of equal length. Draw line AD, with point D the midpoint on line BC. Draw line DE, which makes ADE a right angle.

L-Shape and Square Puzzle

A third puzzle having more than one solution is shown in Figure 3. To construct this puzzle, draw on graph paper a wide L-shape in which lines AB, BC, and FG are of equal length. Lines AG, CD, DE, and EF are each equivalent to one-half the length of line AB. Lines BG and EG intersect at point G.

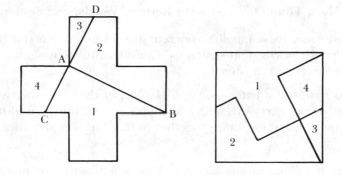

Figure 1. Cross and square puzzle.

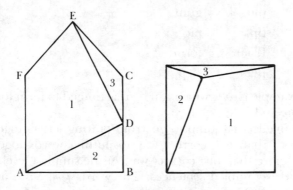

Figure 2. Pentagon and square puzzle.

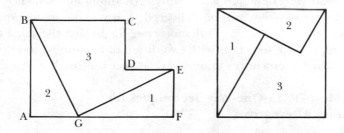

Figure 3. L-shape and square puzzle.

Step 2: More Than One Way with Letters, Words, and Sentences

Let's move from these tangibly concrete puzzles to less concrete items, such as letters, words, and sentences. Consider this exercise, to which there are two correct answers:

> You have three letters—*o, n, t*. If you put them together as *nto*, they do not carry meaning and do not form a word found in the dictionary. Put the letters together so that they *do* carry meaning.
>
> Answer: *not, ton*

Just as the same puzzle pieces can be put together to make two different shapes, the same letters can be arranged to make two different words. Here are other examples of letter combinations that can be arranged more than one way:

1. apl	lap	pal
2. mgu	mug	gum
3. pti	tip	pit
4. ofmr	from	form
5. tpes	pets	step

A sixth example is *ostp*, which can be rearranged to form four words: *spot, tops, stop,* and *pots*.

It's a big intellectual jump to go from putting letters together into words in more than one correct way to putting words together into sentences in more than one correct way. At the simplest level, children can work with scrambled sentences. The words *Jim, Susie,* and *chased* can be put together as *Jim chased Susie* or as *Susie chased Jim*. The same three words form two different sentences that are equally "correct" but different in meaning.

At a more complex level, a sentence can be put together in more than one correct way by punctuation. *Mother said Mary* can become *"Mother," said Mary* or *Mother said, "Mary."* An ambiguous sentence, such as *Students are revolting,* can be delivered with varying intonation patterns and facial expressions to demonstrate again that the same three words can produce sentences with two different meanings. You can use puns and double entendres to develop the idea still further.

Step 3: More-Than-One-Way Techniques for Generating Alternatives

Steps 1 and 2 have encouraged pupils to *find* more than one answer. The next step is to help each pupil *generate* more than one answer. You want to develop open-ended thinking to the point where pupils can come up with alternatives and maybe even choose from among the alternatives.

Again you can start with tangible, concrete objects, such as those used in still-life paintings. Put such objects as an apple, a book, a scarf, a vase, and some flowers on the table. Ask each student to work out three different arrangements of these objects. If you want to progress to the idea of choosing from among alternatives, you can have each student decide which arrangement he or she likes best. After classmates have seen the three arrangements, they can vote for the one they like best. Sometimes the student's favorite differs from the classmates' top choice, which provides another example of more than one answer.

Sociodramas can help students learn to generate multiple alternatives for a simulated real-life situation. In the following transcription of a sociodrama concerning the selection of a birthday present, the initial conversation shows that these students are able to do open-ended thinking. They take the time to generate many alternatives before they even approach a decision.

> *Cliff:* I wish we had more than a dollar each to spend on Michael's birthday present. You can't get much for a dollar.
>
> *Rocky:* All three of us could put our money together for one present. Then we'd have three dollars.
>
> *Candy:* Or we could split up the money for one two-dollar present and one one-dollar present.
>
> *Cliff:* What do you think Michael wants? We can't decide how to split the money until we figure out what we're going to give him.
>
> *Candy:* How about a ball or a book or a game?
>
> *Rocky:* Or candy or a bat or balloons?
>
> *Cliff:* Let's make a list of everything we can think of that he might like. Then we can start narrowing down. . . .

Compositions often reflect how children have progressed from one-way thinking to open-ended thinking, as demonstrated in this sixth grader's story:

> The volcano erupted. Cindy and Laurie saw the lava coming. Laurie just ran. She was a one-way thinker. She couldn't think of anything to do but run. The lava ran faster than Laurie, so that was the end of her.
> Cindy was a more-than-one-way thinker. When she saw the lava coming, she climbed a tree. The lava piled up higher, so she swung

over to a roof. It got higher still, so she waved to a helicopter and it picked her up.

MORAL: You've got a better chance if you are a more-than-one-way thinker.

And as a teacher, you've got a better chance for open-ended discussions if you promote more-than-one-way thinking.

Reference

Leeming, Joseph. *Fun with Puzzles*. Philadelphia: J. P. Lippincott, 1946.

Critical Thinking through a Community of Inquiry

Kristine Riemann[1]
Alamo Heights Junior School, San Antonio, Texas

Tony W. Johnson
University of Texas at San Antonio

"I'd like to make a rebuttal to Anne's comment."

This remark could have been made by a college student participating in a philosophy seminar or by a high school student engaged in a forensic debate. In fact, it is a statement made by Jason, one of my sixth-grade students.

Critical Thinking in the Classroom

Early in the school year my sixth-grade language arts class began using the novel *Harry Stottlemeier's Discovery* as a vehicle for developing a critical approach to learning. In chapter one of the novel, Harry, a ten-year-old boy, becomes interested in how rearranging sentences affects their meaning. He learns, for example, that true statements such as "all cucumbers are vegetables" become false when reversed to "all vegetables are cucumbers." My students were intrigued over whether Harry discovered or invented the rule that a true *all* statement becomes false when reversed. To help them explore the differences between a discovery and an invention, I used an exercise from the teacher's manual accompanying the novel.

The class generally agreed that a discovery is something you "know, but can't prove." As Sam suggested, a discovery is "already there and you just find it." They were willing to accept electricity and America as examples of discoveries. Invention, on the other hand, they defined as something not already in existence. Again Sam added clarification by remarking that invention takes "the pieces that are already there and builds something new from them." The class accepted the electric light, television, and soap as examples of invention.

121

The class quickly focused on one item for discussion. Determining whether the development we call a *city* was a discovery or an invention piqued their interest, noisily dividing the class. On the side of discovery, a few students offered explanations that are summarized below:

> Elaina: People didn't plan who would be whose neighbor.
>
> Chris: The city just came into being as settlements spread; people came together because they needed jobs; buildings were built.
>
> Julie: Populations in certain places grew by coincidence and *then* people instituted a government.

A much larger—and less unified—group espoused the position of city as invention. The following summations exemplify the students' responses:

> Monty: A city was preplanned; someone brought people to the existing land and used the existing resources to make something new. (Monty supported his position with the example of an eastern settlement developed by Ethan Allen.)
>
> John and Roger: People did not just happen to build next to one another; rather, they *chose* to build near each other.

Mark proposed that the core issue seemed to be whether a governing body decided to build a city (invention) or whether a city just grew and then people set up their government (discovery). At this point, the level of disagreement was so high that the students asked me if we could take some time to research the issue and have an informal debate. Delighted by their enthusiasm, I agreed. Students used our class library time and their own time outside of class to read encyclopedia and other reference articles and to ask questions of parents, social studies teachers, and friends.

When their research was completed, class time was set aside for each of the opposing factions to meet and consolidate its information. The smaller "discovery" group immediately elected a chairperson and quietly organized its defense. The larger "invention" group spent a good deal of time arguing loudly over who would be in charge and how they would proceed. Three subgroups evolved and finally set to work. I watched as the two groups prepared for the debate.

As a class, we decided on the format of the debate. Each side would be allowed two to three minutes for a representative to present facts and reasons that supported that group's point of view. Then two other representatives would be allowed to follow up these points, argue for their side, and add any relevant details. The students requested that we invite our school counselors to attend so that there would be a wider audience for the debate.

The debate itself was run with efficiency and dignity. Both sides presented sound arguments and solid support for their positions. No clear winner emerged, but the whole class obviously gained. We had experienced education as it should occur—teacher directed, but not dictated, and solidly student centered. It was a delightful way to meet several reading, writing, oral communication, and study skill objectives from our curriculum guide.

The Philosophy for Children Approach

Harry Stottlemeier's Discovery is the first and most widely used of the Philosophy for Children novels developed by Matthew Lipman, director of the Institute for the Advancement of Philosophy for Children.[2] In the 1960s Lipman, then a professor of philosophy at Columbia University, became increasingly alarmed at his college students' inability to understand and follow the rules of reason, and he realized that students needed help in developing their reasoning skills long before their college years. He decided to try using the novel as the medium for introducing children to both the formal and informal rules of thought and wrote *Harry Stottlemeier's Discovery* as a child might tell the story. For more than a decade, Lipman has been a pioneer in the critical thinking skills movement. In addition to the *Harry* program for fifth and sixth graders discussed here, Lipman has developed critical thinking skills programs for younger children (the *Kio and Gus* and the *Pixie* programs) and sequels to the *Harry* program for adolescents. All programs are based on the assumption that children's natural inquisitiveness is their main tool for making sense out of their world. Yet formal education often squelches this natural sense of wonder.

When I first learned of the Philosophy for Children approach (Brandt 1982), I realized that this program would enhance my efforts at helping students develop their critical thinking skills. I have now used the *Harry* novel for two years and can report that it has fostered active student involvement and has aided the development of their higher-level thinking.

Designing the Ideal School

To some degree, my students identified with Harry and other characters in the novel. Specifically, my students had wondered about the importance of what they were learning and were drawn to an episode in *Harry* focusing on why we are in school in the first place. In the episode, Mark Jahorski, one of Harry's friends, gets angry at his teachers for "always trying to fill my mind full of all sorts of junk. . . ." Harry, Mark, and Mark's sister, Maria, engage in a conversation about adults, particularly teachers, and why they behave as they do. Mark claims that all courses and all schools are bad because of "grown-ups." Maria, uncomfortable with Mark's assertion, adds that "someone has to run the schools, and so it has to be the grown-ups, because they know more than anyone else." As the conversation continues, Harry points out that it is not a question of whether grown-ups or kids should run the schools, but whether schools should be run by people who know what they're doing or by people who don't know what they're doing.

My students became intrigued with the question of whether grownups, including teachers, really do know what kids need in order to learn. They insisted that much of what we do in school is a waste of time. In response to my question of how to make school better, students decided to design an ideal school.

The class began to discuss the characteristics of an ideal school. Each student prepared a list of the things such a school requires. Working individually and in small groups, the students began the process of sifting out silly and superfluous ideas and reaching consensus on major points. They soon realized that their lists lacked both depth and consistency. Items ranged from less homework to a larger lunch menu and from bigger lockers to free taxi passes. As one boy pointed out, "We're arguing about the color of the carpet and we haven't even built the building."

Frustrated with their lack of progress, the students agreed to establish goals first and then to proceed accordingly. After lengthy and heated deliberations, the class concluded that the primary goal should be for "more useful learning to take place than the average junior school provides." The class enthusiastically agreed that while learning facts is important, it is equally important to develop the ability to use those facts.

Having established the goals, students began investigating various other aspects of their ideal school. New committees were formed to determine the role of teachers and administrators, to examine equipment and building needs, to develop academic and special subjects, to select books and other materials, and to decide upon grading and discipline procedures. Students tended to be much rougher on themselves in grading and discipline than they would ever allow us teachers to be.

Students began to see that conclusions reached by one committee affected the work of other committees. Through this process they came to an understanding of the complexity of schooling and gained an appreciation for the difficulty that parents, teachers, and administrators face in coordinating the many facets of education. The interest generated by this project sustained itself over three months of active student involvement, and Harvard Junior School (the name selected by the students) became a paper reality. An eleven-page booklet about the school took form on one student's word processor and was admired by all.

Discussing the Mind and the Brain

In the Philosophy for Children novels, intellectual inquiry almost always occurs in a public place with two or more children engaged in a conversation about something that is puzzling them. The discussion is usually initiated by a character who encounters a confusing situation and seeks help from friends to figure it out. While the problem itself is usually philosophical in nature, the children's manner of coping with it is of more significance. Naively sharing their sense of wonder, these children demonstrate a willingness to express their most private thoughts, to admit their own ignorance or bewilderment, and to overcome their fear of being different, foolish, or stupid. In this manner, children in the novel model for students in the classroom a genuine community of inquiry.

For example, a conversation in the *Harry* novel about the workings of the mind led to a thoughtful classroom discussion about the mind and the brain. Although I did not ask for metaphors or analogies (both recently studied), students' remarks included some clever figures of speech:

> Anne said that the mind is a TV and that people change their thinking by turning to a new channel.

> Justin saw the mind as an invisible place in the brain that stores information. Jay wanted us to be somewhat more specific, calling the mind a part of the brain that stores memories or thoughts.

> Mark contended that the brain is for thinking and the mind for dreaming.

> Chris likened the brain to a library and the mind to the pages of the books in the library.

> Rusty called the brain spaghetti surrounded by meat sauce and the mind the smart part of the spaghetti.

As with our discussion of discovery and invention, the students were stimulated to learn more. Twenty-three library books on the mind, the brain, and related topics were displayed in the classroom for a week, and students browsed through them during study time. Many showed me passages that supported their points of view or shed new light on something that had puzzled them. Often students would share their insights or thoughts with other students. Our classroom was transformed into a community of inquiry in which we taught one another and became colleagues investigating important issues together.

A Sense of Community

This sense of community was one of the major benefits my students and I gained from using the Philosophy for Children approach. For the first time in thirteen years of teaching, I found myself orchestrating learning rather than selling it. My students spent time searching for ways to apply what we were currently learning to other questions. Beyond that, students began finding relationships between stories read early in the year and those read much later. They took pride in discovering the ways our language arts subjects fit together and how concepts carried over from subject to subject. Students comfortably challenged me to show how lessons such as diagramming sentences would improve their minds. And they accepted my explanations because we were jointly approaching the learning task. That level of trust—and its accompanying enthusiasm—promoted a year full of "useful education" where more learning took place than customarily occurs in a sixth-grade classroom.

Notes

1. Kristine Riemann narrates here, but the paper is a collaborative effort with Tony W. Johnson.

2. For more information about teaching children philosophy, write to The Institute for the Advancement of Philosophy for Children, Montclair State College, Upper Montclair, NJ 07043.

Reference

Brandt, Anthony. "Teaching Kids to Think." *Ladies Home Journal*, September 1982, 104–106.

Advertising Gimmicks:
Teaching Critical Thinking

Leah Rudasill
Belton High School, Belton, Texas

We live in a world full of color, movement, bright music, and slogans that our young people remember more easily than the names of their cousins across town. They often have a difficult time separating advertisements from "the real thing." Despite our protests, children know that no one can argue with a taste test. Special jeans do attract the opposite sex, and a futuristic scooter will speed them ahead of their friends. As Donald Tutolo (1981, 680) writes, students give credibility to the concepts that they hear and see the most. But with our assistance, students can learn to think carefully about advertising.

My English I high school students and I study advertising propaganda—how and why we all get "suckered" by products and promises. In a three-week unit, we examine the advertising gimmicks used in magazines and on television. Students have fun during the unit, but at the same time they are utilizing such high-level thinking skills as critical thinking, analysis, methods of persuasion, assimilation, creation, and evaluation, and are getting practice in writing and speaking.

I introduce the unit with a short quiz in which students identify often heard advertising slogans, such as the following:

1. Oh, what a feeling!
2. Where's the beef?
3. Kills roaches dead.
4. The choice of the new generation.
5. The Breakfast of Champions.
6. Reach out and touch someone.
7. Don't leave home without it.
8. The cheese that goes crunch.
9. Snap! Crackle! Pop!
10. The Uncola.

127

Most of the slogans are familiar to students. Through repeated exposure, they have become today's advertising experts.

After the quiz, we discuss the different tricks advertisers use to catch and keep an audience. The students brainstorm types of gimmicks, such as the following nine categories:

1. *Sex Appeal:* The use of sex to sell a product.
2. *Snob Appeal:* The consumer will join the ranks of the elite by using the product.
3. *Appeal to Tradition:* The manufacturer says to the consumer, "We have made the best product for over one hundred years." Experience is the key.
4. *Appeal to Authority:* This selling device depends on a spokesperson, a television star, a well-known athlete, or a public figure to endorse the item. Use of the product will make the consumer as wealthy, famous, talented, or beautiful as the spokesperson.
5. *Outright Propaganda:* If the consumer does not buy this product, he or she will become a social outcast.
6. *Plain Folks:* Reverse snob appeal applies here. "Good ol' boys like us believe in plain, good-quality items. None of this fancy stuff."
7. *Something for Nothing, or More for Less:* This gimmick suggests a product is of better quality than its higher-priced competitors.
8. *Appeal to Excellence:* This gimmick closely relates to snob appeal. "Only the best is good enough for me."
9. *Everyone Else Has One:* This technique is effective with most of us, who don't want to stand out by being different.

After my advertising experts have identified a list of tricks, they form groups of three or four students. I provide paper, scissors, tape, and a stack of magazines for each group. Their assignment is to find and cut out at least two examples of each gimmick on the list. The ads are then grouped to make a book, with the particular advertising technique identified on the back of each page. By the end of three days, most groups have completed their books.

A closer look at television advertising is the next step in this unit promoting critical thinking. For one or two class periods, we view commercials videotaped from prime-time television programs. We discuss again the tricks used to hook the consumer. By this time, the students are quick to identify the particular psychological persuasion used. As experts, the young people are fascinated by viewing the ads in a new light.

After this minireview, students form small groups of two or three students. Their assignment this time is to write a commercial. The groups spend several days drafting and discussing ideas, and then each group selects one product to advertise. The students write the script for the ad, including dialogue, setting, and a description of what the camera will see. They rehearse their commercials during the next class period, and on the following day I videotape the commercials.

At this point the students need to review the purpose of the assignment because most have been intent on producing a commercial that was either funny or cute, without realizing that they, in every case, used the same persuasive techniques found in the professional ads. As we watch the students' commercials and laugh, we analyze the techniques used. The revelation that they borrowed the advertisers' gimmicks for their own ads shocks my students and drives home the lesson.

Simple exposure to the psychological "hooks" present in these advertisements makes students aware of the role that critical thinking should play in their lives. In his classic exploration of advertising, Vance Packard (1957, 3) warned that "large-scale efforts are being made, often with impressive success, to channel our unthinking habits, our purchasing decisions, and our thought processes." It is essential that we teach young people to analyze what they see and hear. The business of manipulating minds becomes more commonplace, yet more subtle, every year. Advertising works "by making the consumer hear things that are not being said, accept as truths things that have only been implied, and believe things that have only been suggested" (Tutolo 1981, 680). We must make our students aware of the empty promises of hope, vitality, prestige, and athletic prowess hidden in the ads for beauty cream, orange juice, automobiles, and tennis shoes.

References

Packard, Vance. *The Hidden Persuaders*. New York: David McKay, 1957.

Tutolo, Daniel. "Critical Listening/Reading of Advertisements." *Language Arts* 58, no. 6 (September 1981): 679–83.

The Uses of Logic in the College Freshman English Curriculum

Angela A. Rapkin
Manatee Community College, Bradenton, Florida

The information explosion and the trend toward specialization have placed on the teacher of written communication a tremendous burden to include in the curriculum material that would otherwise be covered in separate courses. Until only a few years ago, many colleges and universities in the country required that all freshmen take a basic course in logic. Today, recognizing the necessary relationship between clear thinking and writing, teachers of freshman English are offering the essence of the logic course as part of a unit on argumentation. Evidence of this ongoing procedure is the number of freshman English texts which continue to include not only a unit on argumentation but a thorough introduction to elementary logic as well: definitions of induction, deduction, the syllogism, enthymeme, evidence, proof, validity, and logical fallacies, with clever examples and exercises for each of these.[1]

The Initial Logic Unit

My own practice has been to begin integrating the logic curriculum early in the course and to continue referring to it whenever it is relevant.[2] As I plan lessons and tests and as I evaluate my students' papers, I pay close attention to logic and am on the lookout for faulty logic. For example, when we approach the cause/effect mode, I caution the students about causal fallacies, and I address three such fallacies at that time:

1. *Post hoc, ergo propter hoc.* I demonstrate this fallacy with the example that shortly after Jane Coed becomes involved with John Doe, Jane drops out of school. Her parents blame her decision on her relationship with John. I ask the students if the parents' assumption is accurate. The students are quick to realize that Jane may

have been failing one or more courses and may have been planning to drop out of school for some time. I relate this to topics of a personal nature that the students may be selecting for their themes and caution them against this type of thinking.

2. Mistaking the nature of the cause. As an example, I use my response, as a new college teacher, to the occasional student who dozed off in my classes. I assumed he or she was inattentive and a poor student, but on examination of the cause, I discovered one student was a single parent raising several children and working as an aid on the night shift at a nearby hospital, and another student had a medical problem requiring him to take a medication which caused drowsiness.

3. Failing to recognize that there may be more than one cause. I exemplify this fallacy by suggesting that it took more than talent alone to make Joe Namath a superior athlete. The athletes in my class add that other causes for his success may be that Namath practiced a great deal, had a good coach, and had excellent family support.

For each of these fallacies, I try to find additional examples in the topics my students select for their cause-and-effect papers, and I encourage them to think through their analysis thoroughly before outlining their thesis points.

The Argumentation Unit

I wait until the end of the semester for the argumentation unit because of its difficulty. By that time the students have a working knowledge of many of the terms pertaining to logic. In an effort to expand their recognition and subsequent avoidance of logical fallacies, I concentrate on some fifteen specific fallacies. I make a personal contribution to these lessons by carefully selecting and editing my own experiences, which I then share as discoveries made spontaneously during class discussion or while planning the lesson (a process I often share with my students). For example, I tell them that my favorite example of the *post hoc* fallacy is one I caught myself making when my thirteen-year-old son suddenly, after months of my nagging him to be more conscientious about his grooming, appeared at the breakfast table with his hair blown dry, his shirt and slacks well coordinated, and his fingernails clean. I mistakenly assumed the *cause* of his changed behavior to be my doing. "I finally got through to this kid," I thought. Then I ask my

class what they think really caused him to change, and several are quick
to call out, "A girl!" to which I promptly respond, "Right. Her name is
Kim."

Next I set up a workshop on logical fallacies in advertising. In the
workshop setting, students must apply their theoretical knowledge to
concrete realities, which, in the case of magazine advertisements, are
often bizarre. It is at this time that the real learning occurs, for the
sequence in which the students are actively involved demands that they
go through several thinking processes. The students are asked to select
two magazine ads from major publications. The ads should appear to
be illogical. I give them only two or three examples, carefully selected
from television commercials no longer being shown. For instance, I ask
them what qualifies Annette Funicello as an expert on peanut butter.
Is it that she was a famous kid, or that she is a mother? This obvious
appeal to authority suggests others like it. I want the students to discover
the best examples, so I limit their responses to my presentation. Also,
those who catch on quickly can easily usurp the opportunity for other
students to discover on their own which commercials seem most foolish
(and there are so many to choose from). The students are to select two
ads which seem not to make sense chiefly because of their incongruity.
I suggest that even though the students may not immediately recognize
what the logical fallacy is, they should trust their instincts and cut out
the ad anyway. I assure them that after we analyze and identify a few
ads in class, they will be able to put the proper name on the error in
their ads.

On the day the ads are due, most students show up with a folder full
of ads and share them with interest, curiosity, and great humor.
Certainly it is illogical to see that tall, skinny woman in her bra and
panties standing in the bull pen of that baseball field. But what is the
formal name of such a silly juxtaposition? To facilitate a written
discussion analyzing their ads, I provide each student with a worksheet.
First the students are to select one ad and to write a brief description
of it. This is not only good practice in writing description, but it also
forces students to articulate and focus on what it is about the ad that is
offensive to their sense of logic. Second, I ask the students to name the
fallacy (or fallacies) which they think are present in the ad. Finally, I
ask the students to explain the errors in logic. They are to put into
words what the images in the ad suggest to the consumer—in what way
is this unsound and misleading?

As the students select their ads and try to complete the assignment,
I walk around the room and show the disgust, amazement, incredulity,
and good humor that the ads elicit. I hold up the ads that I consider

to be the real winners and ask the class questions about the relationship between the people and objects in the ad and the item being advertised. For example, I find it "fascinating" that the advertisers for Maidenform underwear promise women they'll always be "in control of the situation in sleek, sensuous Sweet Nothings." And to demonstrate this, they picture the tall, skinny "Maidenform Woman" clothed in a bra and matching bikini with a luxurious red and gold cape trailing down her back, a crown on her head, and a whip in her hand; she is in a circus arena directing a tiger through a fiery hoop. ("You never know where she'll turn up!") Surely there are certain causal fallacies operating here. If a woman wears this underwear, she will not automatically find herself "in control of the situation." Further, control is gained by means other than "sleek, sensuous" underwear. Finally, there appears to be a false analogy here: does the ad suggest that a woman in "sleek, sensuous" underwear can control a man just as a circus performer controls a tiger trained to jump through a fiery hoop?

Another example of a fallacy in logic that my students have spotted is a double-page ad for Jag sportswear. On the top of the left page it says, "Nothing but. . . ." In the upper right-hand corner of the next page it says, "Jag, Jeans and Sportswear." If the words don't give away the false dilemma, the picture will. Across the double page is a picture of an elegant dinner party. All of the guests are nude—except for the waiters, who are attired in tuxedos, and one young lady who is, of course, attired in Jag sportswear and who has attracted the attention of all the men. Interesting. Another causal fallacy: if women wear Jag sportswear, they will get the undivided attention of all the men.

Each discussion results in a serious designation of the type of fallacy, so the students are really working together on the assignment. The most common fallacies which are used in pictorial ads include the bandwagon, faulty either/or statements, false analogies, and causal fallacies. Advertisements promise incredible results from using particular products. "Vantage, The taste of success." Clean teeth and a bright smile result in a marvelous romance. Use a Canon T70 and you'll take "great shots" as easily as Larry Bird shoots baskets. And, of course, we all know how to get a great pair of legs.

The students begin to catch on and recognize these fallacies quickly. One confusing ad shows Martina Navratilova holding up her Wimbledon trophy. On the arm of her sweater, "ComputerLand" has been sewn. The big print reads, "This year you can win Wimbledon!" Beneath it the smaller print reads, "Through your ComputerLand store." This is a sweepstakes contest, and the grand prize is a trip for two to Wimbledon. The obvious causal fallacy degenerates into a hopeless analogy: just as there's only one number one in women's tennis, there's only one number one computer store, ComputerLand. In another ad, a tequila manufacturer promises that "Anything can happen" if we drink their brand. They picture a group of beautiful young people on a beach in the evening. They all have big smiles. But why would there be three women and two men? Is the ad directed toward men, who are supposed to "jump on the bandwagon" and put themselves in the picture? And then there are those glittering generalities: Anheuser-Busch writes, "Here's to You, America" over frosted bottles of its eight types of beer lined up on ice. Beneath them is written, "Somebody still cares about quality." American Airlines pictures a huge birthday cake topped off by the Statue of Liberty holding a flaming torch and surrounded by airline employees; the caption reads, "You can blow out the candles, but you can never blow out the flame."

Conclusions

My students are generally conscientious. If I asked them to memorize the definitions of fifteen logical fallacies, either to recognize the terms in a matching exercise on an objective test, or to write out word for word on a short essay test, they would dutifully do this. Naturally, I recognize that those two testing situations would demonstrate nothing about the students' ability to think, to make important connections, or to discriminate between alternatives, so I do not test their understanding of the fallacies in either of those two traditional testing modes. Instead, I use the advertising workshop. Students search out the ads with logical fallacies; in writing and in discussion they identify and explain the fallacies present. Their writing usually reveals some further interesting observations as the students invariably select highly connotative words to express their feelings about these ads. In addition, from time to time I make up a sheet of statements—some based on class discussion, some on the news, and some on new ads—and I ask the students to identify and discuss the errors in logic in these statements.

With such practice, I believe that students can avoid making errors in logic, and they can avoid being taken advantage of or manipulated in their daily lives by someone exploiting the subtleties of these logical fallacies. Yes, I do believe that we should be logical and, more important, that the ability to be a critical thinker helps us have a better life.

Notes

1. English teachers have always recognized that good writing requires good thinking, but we have not always known how to improve students' cognitive skills. For an excellent discussion of the relationship between studying formal logic and writing argumentation well, see David S. Kaufer and Christine M. Neuwirth, "Integrating Formal Logic and the New Rhetoric: A Four-Stage Heuristic," *College English* 45, no. 4 (April 1983): 380–89. Their stated purpose is "to suggest that formal logic has more to contribute to argumentation than recent theory and pedagogy would lead us to believe" (380).

2. I keep three resources on reserve for my students: *The Language of Argument* by Daniel McDonald (Harper and Row, 1975), *Strategies of Rhetoric* by A. M. Tibbetts and Charlene Tibbetts (Scott, Foresman, 1974), and *The Art of Thinking: A Guide to Critical and Creative Thought* by Vincent Ryan Ruggiero (Harper and Row, 1984). From time to time I recommend specific pages to supplement our course work, and if certain students are either having difficulties or demonstrate a keen interest, I make specific assignments for reading and exercises in these works.

5 Speaking and Writing Activities across the Curriculum

Helping Students Write Historical Fiction

Myra Zarnowski
Queens College, City University of New York

For several years I have been teaching a combined course in English and American history to seventh-grade students. My favorite project each year has been helping students write historical fiction that complements our "factual" study. I imagine it is the element of surprise that keeps me interested in this project. I'm curious to see how students will manipulate historical events—what they will choose to emphasize and what they will ignore. I want to know what they find surprising and worthy of elaboration. I want a window on their thinking.

Students find the writing of historical fiction a challenging yet rewarding endeavor. First, in order to write a piece of historical fiction, students must know a great deal about the events and people they are describing. With this knowledge comes the satisfaction of being an expert on a particular topic. Second, students take on powerful positions as authors of historical fiction by altering history a bit here and a bit there. Here is a chance to be creative, to explore the "what if" possibilities. The only constraint is that the narrative must be developed logically.

Excerpts from Student Writing

Before explaining the procedure I follow in the classroom, I would like to demonstrate the flavor of this type of writing with two short excerpts from stories written by students. Notice that each excerpt clearly is based on an historical event, yet it also contains fictional elements. Even in these short excerpts, the writers have established engaging narrative situations.

The first excerpt comes from the beginning of a story about the Battle of Lexington. Although it is reminiscent of Howard Fast's novel *April Morning*, it nevertheless manages to draw the reader into the distressing situation of a young boy who is confronting war for the first time. As the boy relates both his thoughts and his remembered experiences, there are numerous possibilities for the writer to elaborate on the sights, sounds, and events of the battle.

> I gripped the [gun] stock, holding on to it for dear life. A shaky hand mopped my sweat-soaked brow. I was surprised to see that the shaky hand was my own. A buzzing sound arose in my ears and there was a lump in my throat. I guess I was scared. I stumbled and almost fell, but Captain David caught me. "You all right boy?" Captain David muttered.
>
> "I'm O.K.," I replied. But I wasn't. I wanted to throw down my musket and run away. I wanted to scream and warn everybody that there were armed British at the North Bridge, but everybody already knew that.

The second excerpt comes from a story about Thomas Jefferson that takes place in a boardinghouse where he is drafting the Declaration of Independence. While it is true that Jefferson wanted to include a section about slavery in the Declaration, the character of Toby, a slave, is completely fictitious.

> In the next couple of days Mr. Jefferson an' me became good friends.
>
> I knocked on the door.
>
> "Toby?"
>
> "Yes, sir. Can I come in?"
>
> "*May I* come in? And, yes, *you may*." I walked in. "Have a seat, Toby. I have to ask you a few questions." I sat on the big wooden chair next to Mr. Jefferson. On his lap was the lap desk that he himself made.
>
> "Mr. Tom, you writin' today?" I hoped the answer would be yes, 'cause I wanted to help.
>
> "Yes, Toby, and I'm glad you're here. I need your opinion. In the Declaration, I want to put something in on the slave trade. To really show the people slavery is a bad thing. But, Toby, I don't want to put the blame on the colonies. Do you understand?"
>
> "Yes, Mr. Tom. Do you want to insult the King? . . ."
>
> "I surely do, Toby. He has enslaved, in a way, all of the colonies with his crazy rule, I . . ."
>
> "Excuse me, but sir, then blame him f . . ."
>
> "That's it, Toby! I'll blame the King for all of our slavery!! I'll . . . yes, he brought slavery to this country!"
>
> "Thank you, Mr. Tom." I felt happy. He understood how I felt. He grabbed his quill pen and scribbled wildly.

During a writing conference, the author of the Jefferson story told me that she was surprised that, in the end, the Founding Fathers did not include mention of slavery or slaves in their demands for equality and freedom. She elaborated this fact in her story. The students I have worked with frequently raise significant issues like this one because they have had time to study their subjects in depth and to develop some expertise. Their writing reveals the serious thinking they have done on the topic.

Project Description

In order to help students write historical fiction, I have them follow a definite procedure: (1) reading and discussing relevant published historical fiction as part of the ongoing literature curriculum, (2) researching a topic in American history, (3) writing a report on that topic, and (4) using information from the report to write historical fiction. This series of steps is an example of *scaffolding* (Applebee and Langer 1983)—that is, one experience facilitating another. In this case, reading, discussing, researching, and reporting provide the background necessary for story writing. The entire project takes from four to six weeks.

Step 1: Reading and Discussing Historical Fiction

Throughout the year, I select novels to complement the topics in American history that we are studying. These novels are discussed by students in small groups and often form the basis of writing assignments. My hope is that students will learn about historical fiction by reading it and, ultimately, will appreciate the work of historical fiction writers through their own writing.

I have used the following novels in conjunction with a unit on early American history:

> *Light in the Forest* by Conrad Richter
>
> *The Witch of Blackbird Pond* by Elizabeth Speare
>
> *The Hessian* by Howard Fast
>
> *April Morning* by Howard Fast
>
> *My Brother Sam Is Dead* by James L. Collier and Christopher Collier
>
> *Johnny Tremain* by Esther Forbes

Step 2: Researching a Topic in American History

Students are asked to select a topic related to our study of early American history. Although I give a list of suggested topics, I will consider students' suggestions. Students are asked to research their topic in depth, using a minimum of four sources. Most of the reading and subsequent notetaking is done in class, giving me the opportunity to observe and help. During research periods, I hold conferences with students in order to discuss their reading and to help them locate appropriate sources. Approximately one and a half hours each day is devoted to research and writing for a period of two to three weeks.

Step 3: Writing the Report

Once their notes are completed, students plan their reports by first listing their topics in order. I require that students use an interesting, attention-grabbing beginning, include at least one quotation, and list all their sources in a bibliography. More significantly, students are encouraged to give their personal reactions to what they have researched. In the following excerpt from a report on the Boston Tea Party, the student tells why he thinks the act was effective:

> There have been many brave and effective acts of rebellion in America's history, but not many compare to the bravery and effectiveness of the Boston Tea Party. In fact, around one hundred and seventy-five Boston craftsmen and farmers banded together to express their feelings at the Boston Tea Party. The fact that Britain even passed the Port Act in reaction to the Tea Party proves that Britain was a little worried. The Boston Tea Party also set an example for other acts of rebellion.

Students do most of their writing in class, where they can get feedback from other readers. In our classroom the availability of five computers has made both writing and revising much easier for many students. Students generally make several printouts before they are completely satisfied with their final reports.

Step 4: Writing Historical Fiction

With their notes and completed reports in hand, students next plan their historical fiction according to three basic steps:

1. *Creating a Character:* Each student creates a character who will play a major role in the story. This character will know real historical figures and will participate in real historical events researched by the student. During the planning stage, the student writes a short character description.

2. *Selecting Factual Information:* Each student selects five to ten pieces of factual information from his or her report that are to be included in the story.

3. *Summary:* Each student briefly summarizes his or her idea for a story. It is understood, however, that this summary is subject to change.

During this project many students find that keeping a process journal is extremely helpful. Here they record daily progress, jot down ideas that might be useful later, react to readings, or try out ideas for reports or stories. (See Zarnowski [1984] for a sample of student journal writing.)

Next students are ready to write their historical fiction. As they write, they confer with me and with their classmates. The revising and editing continue until the stories are in final form.

Benefits of Writing Historical Fiction

Writing historical fiction involves students in our history and that of other countries. It gives students a chance to learn about events and conflicts in depth and then to "get inside" the drama of the event by elaborating and modifying it. Historical figures come to life as students consider the motivations and ideas of people from other eras. What could be more exciting than the drama of historical events?

References

Applebee, Arthur N., and Judith A. Langer. "Instructional Scaffolding: Reading and Writing as Natural Language Activities." *Language Arts* 60, no. 2 (February 1983): 168–75.

Zarnowski, Myra. "What Katy Knew: Clues from a Student Journal." *The English Record* 35 (Third Quarter 1984): 2–4.

Exposing the Edge of Thought: Taking Risks with Expressive Language

Denise Stavis Levine
Fordham University, New York, and New York City
    Public Schools

Title of Project: Seeds

Problem: Effect of high and low temperatures on seed germination

Brief Description: I am going to test and explain the effect temperature has on lima beans. I am using my refrigerator and my room as the test [sites].

Ricky—2/2/85

I had asked the members of my eighth-grade science class to select a question or problem for investigation which would tap their knowledge of scientific concepts and processes. Students were encouraged to work alone or in pairs and to discuss their problems and difficulties with one another. After ten weeks, they were to present an oral report along with any documentation they accumulated. A question-and-answer period or class discussion would follow each presentation. Above is the abstract with which Ricky began his sojourn into the world of scientific problem solving.

Like Frank Smith (1975) and others (Kelly 1969; Pope 1982), I have long believed that children are scientists and problem solvers by nature. As they grapple with the task of making sense of their environment— and, more generally, the world—they form hypotheses about problems facing them and then test these hypotheses in order to construct a "theory of the world in the head" (Smith 1975). In classroom practice, science teachers can capitalize on this natural process by placing pupils at the center of learning, by integrating problem-solving skills with the curriculum at hand, and by supporting students' expressive, heuristic language. It is this expressive function which James Britton refers to as "the exposed edge of thought," stating "whether we write or speak, expressive language is associated with a relationship of mutual confidence and trust and is therefore a form of discourse that encourages us to *take risks,* to try out ideas we are not sure of. . . . In other words, expressive language (as a kind of bonus) is a form that favours exploration, discovery, learning" (1982, 124).

The science projects, then, were an opportunity for students to explore not just a scientific problem but scientific processes as well, an opportunity to think, to predict, to analyze, and, finally, borrowing Jerome Bruner's phrase, to " 'go meta' . . . to turn around on yourself, to reflect upon your reflections" (1984, 1, 6).

Ricky knew, from previous discussions, labs, and films about the work of scientists, that it was important to keep a log for his experiment. He also had some very tentative understanding of "variables" and how these might affect experimental validity. But for Ricky, the significant learning and application of these concepts only came *after* his oral presentation and discussion with his classmates.

Some ten weeks after the initial assignment was given, Ricky volunteered to present his project to the class. He had prepared a large poster on oaktag stating his *problem, hypothesis* ("Room temperatured lima beans would sprout first"), *materials* ("two plastic cups, lima beans"), and *conclusions* ("The low temperatured lima beans were quicker to change and split faster and turned darker on the outside. The room temperatured lima beans were slower in turning colors [rotting] and peeling. The last week these lima beans finally opened."). He added a drawing to give shape and color to his written description and showed the class his weekly log. Ricky pointed out that the cold temperature caused the beans in the refrigerator to rot and decay, as evidenced by the brown color and peeling. This process took longer for the beans at room temperature, which sprouted after five weeks. He spoke about his log increasing his reliability since others could copy his work and see if they got the same results.

Then, the discussion began. Alan pointed out that there was a problem with Ricky's validity since one set of beans received light and the other set (those in the refrigerator) did not. He suggested we could not really tell if it was the light or the warmer temperature which caused the lima beans at room temperature to do better. Initially Ricky responded by saying, "No, my room doesn't really get much sun, so that was okay." But as other students joined in the conversation, Ricky realized that even the indirect daylight for a few hours a day was significantly more light than the beans in the refrigerator had received. The students brainstormed about other places in the house which might allow the same intermittent, short bursts of light as the refrigerator, while still maintaining "room temperature." They realized this was a significant variable that needed to be controlled, and they finally settled on the closet in Ricky's room.

Next, classmates began to question the precise temperature of these two sites. Ricky estimated his room temperature was between 68°F and 74°F most of the time, but he had "no idea" of the temperature in his refrigerator and wondered how we could find that out. This question led another student to suggest that a refrigerator thermometer, available in most hardware stores, would make it easy to note the temperature so that others could better replicate the work.

Ricky seemed pleased with his presentation and the suggestions of his classmates. His next task was to write a clarity statement about what he had learned from the science project, his presentation, and the class discussion. It was time to "go meta," and here's what he wrote:

> 5/9/85
> My project was the effect of room and low temperature on lima beans. My procedure was first I put the lima beans in separate cups then I put one cup in my refrigerater and the other in my room. Then I started a log week by week and when my project was finished I had a poster and a log. My log increased my reliability because it states what happened each week. My vilidity could have been higher if no sun would have gotten to the lima beans in my room, which was pointed out by Alan, or if I knew the temperature in my refrigerater. I learned a lot about doing projects and I am now not afraid to go up in front of the class anymore.

This last sentence indicates the risk that Ricky took in going before his peers to make his presentation. Clearly taking the risk and having confidence in his peers paid off because he had "learned a lot" about scientific processes, specifically validity and reliability, and had discovered perhaps something *more* important about himself: he could speak in front of a group without fear.

Harold Rosen has said that we make new meanings in part "by talking our way toward them" (1969, 128). That, in essence, is what Ricky did. The "meaning-making," making-sense process puts the pupil at the center of his or her learning, and this is the heart of teaching critical thinking. To "go meta" one last time, "in the end, the teacher can only make sense of his pupils making sense" (Rosen 1969, 127).

References

Britton, James. "Language and the Nature of Learning: An Individual Perspective." In *The Teaching of English: 1976 Yearbook of the National Society for the Study of Education*, edited by James Squire. Chicago: National Society for the Study of Education and the University of Chicago Press, 1977.

————. "Notes on a Working Hypothesis about Writing." In *Prospect and Retrospect: Selected Essays of James Britton*, edited by Gordon Pradl. Montclair, N.J.: Boynton/Cook, 1982.

Bruner, Jerome. "Notes on the Cognitive Revolution: OISE's Centre for Applied Cognitive Science." *Interchange* 15, no. 3 (1984): 1–8.

Kelly, George A. *A Theory of Personality: The Psychology of Personal Constructs*. New York: W. W. Norton, 1963.

Pope, Maureen L. "Personal Construction of Formal Knowledge." *Interchange* 13, no. 4 (1982): 3–14.

Rosen, Harold. "Towards a Language Policy across the Curriculum." In *Language: The Learner and the School*. Harmondsworth, England: Penguin Books, 1969.

Smith, Frank. *Comprehension and Learning*. New York: Holt, Rinehart and Winston, 1975.

Math-Writing and Thinking

Adele Fiderer
Scarsdale Public Schools, Scarsdale, New York

Tim

Yash, today we learned about front-ending. Front-ending is estimating. Why? Because 80% percent of math in people's lives is estimating. You still don't know what I mean. I mean if you have this addition problem:

284 -
4,400
9,290
. Focus on the highest place value collumn. You add 9,000 and the 1,000 and you get 10,000 Now you have your estimate answer.

Tim wrote this letter to his friend Yash, a student in another fourth-grade classroom, to explain front-ending, a new way of estimating that he had just learned. Through this four-day letter-writing project, I discovered that writing helped my students think about and learn a new mathematical process. It also led them to integrate common mathematical terms into their speech and writing.

148

To write about the front-ending process, Tim had to use the following critical thinking skills:

> sorting and connecting relevant ideas
>
> sequencing those ideas in a logical way
>
> selecting specific words and terms to clarify meaning
>
> inventing original examples

The Math Lesson

Front-ending is a rough form of estimation in which only the greatest place values are used to arrive at an estimated sum. It's not a difficult concept for fourth graders, and I decided to ask students to explain it in writing for that reason. I would help them develop a pool of rudimentary understandings from which they could later "fish" for ideas and words.

The lesson began with a brief demonstration of the process, followed by practice with several addition problems. I then introduced the writing element by asking my students to write letters to friends in other classrooms describing what they had learned that day. Having a particular audience in mind often released my students' natural voices when they wrote on assigned topics.

"What words do you think you might need to explain front-ending?" I asked. The children recalled words I had used in my demonstration of front-ending, which I listed on the blackboard along with their own suggestions: *column, important, significant number, place value, highest value, estimate, sum, added, digits, zeros, addends, thousands, hundreds.* I assured them, as I did whenever they wrote, that they were free to use any of these words, or their own words, as long as they explained in a clear way how to front-end.

Drafting, Conferring, and Revising

My students began their drafts. They knew that in this stage of writing they needed only to get their ideas on the paper. They were not yet concerned about spelling, handwriting, or the conventions of writing— punctuation, capitalization, and grammar. Carrying over revision strategies from our frequent writing workshops, many crossed out words and phrases and inserted new ones as they wrote. Most drafts were unclear because the writers had not supplied enough information nor used precise words. I was surprised to see that most, like Tim, had invented their own addition problems to help them describe the process.

Tim's first draft was messy. He crossed out and added words as he tried to get his meaning across to Yash. After reading his first draft to his conference partner, Tim learned that one sentence—"Now you add the numbers together"—wasn't clear.

"What numbers are you talking about?" his partner asked.

Tim pointed to the nine and the one, and then wrote on his paper: "You add 9,000 and the 1,000 and you get 10,000."

As my students wrote, I moved quickly from writer to writer, pausing only long enough to ask one or two brief questions, and soon reached Bill's desk. Bill, a student who received help with his reading, math, and language skills in our school's learning center, was having a harder time expressing his ideas about front-ending than was Tim. This is what he had written:

> to Danny Walsh
> We just learned how to front-end. You Have to write a Problem
> down like this.   7,356   You just have to look At
> $$+3,283$$
> 10,000
> the frist 2 highest numbers.

To help Bill make his meaning clearer, I asked, "Bill, you say to look at the first two 'highest numbers.' I'm not sure where they are. Is there a name you can give the place where I'll find those numbers even if the problem is different? Look at the list of words on the blackboard."

Bill looked at the board and answered, "The highest value."

I said, "That's very clear to me now. I understand that I have to add the seven and the three. Can you make that clear in your draft? There's one other thing I don't quite understand. What happens after you add the seven and the three? Is ten your estimated sum?"

Bill thought for a moment before responding; then he explained, "The other columns turn into zeros."

"How?" I pressed. "How do they turn?"

Bill said, "Put zeros under the line under the rest of the columns. I'm going to change that part, too."

Here is Bill's revised description:

> To Danny Walsh
> We just learned how to front-end. You have to write a Problem
> down like this: 7,356   You have to look At the
> $$+3,283$$
> 10,000
> first colome on the left and put zero under line under the rest of
> the coulnm.

Bill was not comfortable with the term *highest value* to indicate the digits that were to be added together. He preferred to identify their location as "the first colome on the left." I believe in the importance of a writer's ownership of a piece, no matter what the form, so I did not interfere with Bill's choices. There are many ways to make the meaning clearer.

But I did continue to gently "prod" him with questions. After the students met with me in small group conferences the next day, Bill deleted the words *look at* and inserted the more specific verb *add* in their place.

Editing

Once students determined their letters were "finished," they were encouraged to search for and correct errors in spelling, punctuation, capitalization, and paragraphs. I did a final proofreading check and returned the letters to students for rewriting on "good" paper in their best handwriting. After recopying, I rarely made additional corrections, even if a few errors remained.

Conclusion

By writing about a new math concept, Bill, Tim, and my other students reaped rewards in the form of a more lasting understanding of a new concept and improved writing skills.

I gained benefits from their writing, too. It opened a window, allowing me to look into their minds and discover what each had learned that day and what I needed to teach the next day. I learned that the same thinking skills that helped them become better writers helped them become better mathematicians as well.

Teaching Critical Thinking to Management Students

Joan M. van Courtland Moon
University of Massachusetts–Boston

College faculty members are not alone in their dismay over the weak reasoning and writing skills they observe in their classrooms. Managers and corporate executives also lament that weakness both in themselves and in those who work for them. One need no more than glance at the many workshops offered by the American Management Association in "Better Business Communications" to sense the need. In an attempt to go beyond the traditional managerial communication course and get at the essential or core reasoning skills that underlie sound thinking and effective writing, the Essential Skills Department in the College of Management at the University of Massachusetts–Boston offers Critical Thinking and Writing courses. These courses were developed in the late 1970s shortly after the college was founded.[1] The college, a public institution whose student population has a median age of twenty-seven, offers a four-year degree in management. The departmental curriculum is based on the premise that thinking skills can be explicitly taught to and learned by adults. We proceed on the notion that most students possess certain core abilities but frequently do not use them. Instead, they often mimic the outcome of those skills. Professors, examining the work without attending to the reasoning process from which it emerges, credit the learners with understanding, when, in truth, students have simply repeated what they have read in the textbook or what the professor has told them. Sometimes a student who is credited with higher-order reasoning skills has simply reiterated a concept learned previously. The student may not be using reasoning skills but is succeeding instead through an impressive display of mimicry. Without these skills, the student fails utterly when invention, rather than reiteration, is called for.

These mental habits or skills, essential to all academic and professional disciplines, include the ability to concentrate, to search for and test alternatives, to break down large and complex problems into smaller parts, to look for analogues when confronting the unfamiliar, and to check the accuracy of the thought process when reaching a conclusion (Whimbey and Lochhead 1982, 11–20; see also Woditsch 1977).

The courses we offer attempt to involve the students actively in their own learning primarily by making them *aware* of how they learn, of their own thinking abilities, of the method they can follow in solving thinking and writing problems, and of the power of language. To that end, we structure classroom situations in which students must verbalize their thoughts. This action enables students, who otherwise are accustomed to thinking silently, to hear themselves and to evaluate what they hear. Of course, it also allows other students and the instructor to listen to their "thoughts-in-progress" and to evaluate these thoughts in light of the reasoning skills noted above. Students then express their ideas, arguments, and conclusions in writing during the class session. This pedagogy allows the instructor to stimulate students' thinking and to observe both the writing-in-process and the final document.

As faculty members in a college of management, we know that our students will have to master both the requirements of academic discourse and those of professional writing. Consequently, we use a strategy in our courses which is calculated to give students guided practice in recognizing and writing definitions, in making inferences based on accurate observation and reporting, and in crafting inductive and deductive arguments and using evidence persuasively. Since we believe that these habits of mind, appropriately developed, ought to prepare students for thoughtful analysis and clear expression, we eschew teaching the traditional business communication models of letter, memo, and report. The skills needed to write a marketing survey, an essay examination question, a term paper, or an annual report are essentially alike, while specific formats are variable and easily learned when the need arises.

An Exercise in Critical Thinking

To get students actively involved in their own learning and to provide us with a "window" on their thinking and writing habits, we divide the class into groups containing three students; one student volunteers to be the scribe for his or her group. To show how this method works, here is an assignment that our management students confront about two-thirds of the way through the semester. Students are given the assignment shown in Figure 1. They are to consider the problem carefully before the next class session, to make some preliminary jottings, and to be prepared to explain to their group the reasons for their conclusions.

Personnel Assignment

This is your first day of work. You have been hired to supervise nine workers who will soon be called on to learn and to operate new computerized phototypesetting machines. Eight of your nine new machines will be delivered in six weeks, but the first machine has just been installed. You must choose an employee to operate the one new model. The existing machines in the shop produce an average of 390 negatives per day. In order to complete the work contracted for the next six weeks, you must average 410 negatives per day. A careful study of the personnel records suggests that four workers are capable of making the transition to the new machine and of attaining the necessary increase in production. Given the following information, which of the following four employees would you select?

	Red Dixon	Tom Fletcher	Dee Sanchez	Edna Waters
Response to training	6	10	7	7
Promotion rating	4	9	8	7
Skill on present machine	10	9	9	8
Health attendance	8	8	9	9
Motivation	5	4	7	8
Average negatives per day	54	36	45	46
Years employed by company	16	3	14	21
Present machine*	A	E	B	B

*A = newest machine with highest production potential, while F = oldest, least productive machine

Red Dixon: Union representative. Red sets a quota which limits productivity of all A and B machines.

Tom Fletcher: Bright, energetic. Tom does excellent work filling in on A and B. He is also respected as the person who is best at troubleshooting problems.

Dee Sanchez: Likes her friends on B and didn't want to move to an A machine when given the opportunity.

Edna Waters: Thinking retirement. Edna is a respected senior employee who solves more personnel problems at the lunch table in a week than union grievance procedures do in a year.

Assignment

1. Deduce two criteria for judging the candidates' qualifications.

2. Construct pro and con arguments for each employee; then indicate your choice to operate the new equipment.

Figure 1. A problem-solving exercise for management students.

In this particular exercise, students are given information—some of it relevant, some of it not. They are asked to interpret that information in light of the central issue, "Who would you select for the job and why?" Before the decision can be made, however, the writer must deduce the criteria by which she or he will judge the candidates' qualifications. After defining the problem, deducing the criteria, sorting out the pertinent data, interpreting the information, and comparing the individuals' qualifications in terms of the established criteria, the students must then craft a pro and con argument for selecting each of the four individuals and, finally, select the one who best fits the criteria.

During the class session, the instructor does much listening and very little speaking. If group members are truly "stuck" or cannot agree on a point, they are to ask the instructor for assistance. That help usually comes in the form of a question. Questions are also asked once each group has reached a decision. For example, most students will select Tom Fletcher as the most appropriate candidate for the job. At this point the instructor asks such questions as: "What are your criteria? Have you defined them carefully? Did you look for the criteria in the numbers? What do these numbers *mean*? Does *10* represent a high or a low value? Have you applied your criteria equally to each candidate, or are you measuring these candidates in terms of each other?" Questioning helps most groups begin to see they have not made a persuasive case. They may have failed to read the opening paragraph carefully. ("What does the company need now? What will it require six weeks from now?") Or they may have ignored the apparent contradictions in the numbers. ("How is it that Fletcher has a *4* in motivation but a *9* in promotion rating?") Some may have made dubious assumptions. ("Can you disqualify Waters because you know that 'she is thinking retirement'?")

In this process, student writers engage in problem-solving activities by identifying the problem, listing the constraints and the assumptions, drawing inferences, and reaching conclusions. They verbalize their thinking, giving their instructor and their peers a chance to intervene in the thinking/writing process.

Students must actively participate; there is no lecture for them to absorb passively. To succeed in the course, students must develop effective group communication skills of listening, paraphrasing, compromising, questioning, and defending their arguments, and they must be both learners and teachers. They draft and redraft their papers and edit the papers for correctness. Then they present these written reports of their activities to their instructor. Through this and similar other guided exercises, students approach the writing of their individual papers for the course with greater confidence and ease.

Utilizing Conceptual Skills

This exercise, similar in its cumulative approach to the other exercises we devise, circles back to call into play important skills addressed earlier in the course: the ability to define, to observe and describe, and to draw inferences and construct inductive arguments. Each class session attempts to engage the student in those essential conceptual skills that analytic writing demands: the ability to focus on a problem, to reflect on the evidence rather than guessing, to test out possible alternatives with patient persistence rather than jumping to conclusions, and to check the accuracy of one's own procedures. The design of the exercises allows the instructor to observe the student's use of these central skills and provides the opportunity to make the student aware of the presence and function of these skills.

Students begin to understand that clear thinking and effective writing are inseparable; refining their thinking requires rewriting. They must be willing "to meet logical contradictions head on and trace them to the premises that have created them" (Swift 1973, 62). Writing becomes a way of thinking that goes beyond the notion of written language simply as a tool of academic or managerial communication. Our management students begin to see how writing enables them to determine what information is needed, select what is relevant, evaluate the evidence, and weave a persuasive argument. The ability to do this not only enhances students' skills as problem solvers and decision makers, but empowers them as critical thinkers, giving them the flexibility and confidence to meet the professional challenges they will encounter.

Note

1. The curriculum was developed by Mark Schlesinger, professor of essential skills at the College of Management, University of Massachusetts–Boston, and by Norman Klein, currently professor of writing at the Harvard Business School. The writing exercise described here was developed by Norman Klein.

References

Swift, Marvin H. "Clear Writing Means Clear Thinking Means. . . ." *Harvard Business Review* 51, no. 1 (January/February 1973): 62.

Whimbey, Arthur, and Jack Lochhead. *Problem Solving and Comprehension*. 3d ed. Philadelphia: Franklin Institute Press, 1982.

Woditsch, Gary A. *Developing Generic Skills*. Bowling Green, Ohio: CUE Project Publications, Bowling Green State University, 1977.